FUNDAMENTALS OF
FUND RAISING

A Primer for Church Leaders

David L. Heetland

DISCIPLESHIP RESOURCES
MATERIALS FOR GROWTH IN CHRISTIAN FAITH AND LIFE
P.O. Box 189 • Nashville, TN 37202 • Phone (615) 340-7284

ISBN 0-88177-082-5

Library of Congress Catalog Card No. 89-90344

DR082B

TO

KATHY, TAMMY, AND TONYA

CONTENTS

PREFACE

The following pages were written to address a concern I have that too many church leaders are not properly trained or motivated to lead congregations toward a stronger stewardship of financial resources. I hope in some small way that these chapters might assist in giving church leaders the background and confidence they need to lead congregations boldly to new levels of understanding and commitment.

I am indebted to many in this effort. I am especially grateful to Garrett-Evangelical Theological Seminary for granting me a three-month study leave so I could devote full time to writing. Thanks also to the development staff for carrying on so admirably in my absence and especially to Barbara Skinner who assisted with much of the research.

Professional fund raising consultants, colleagues in ministry, and laypersons in the church all inspired me with their dedication to stewardship, and their influence permeates each page. A special word of thanks to Fern Underwood, who encouraged me throughout this project, and to Norma Gaskill for her helpful comments and editorial suggestions. Appreciation to the following who also graciously read and critiqued the manuscript: Fran Alguire, Philip Bash, Neal Fisher, David Scoates, and Russell Weigand.

Most of all I wish to express my appreciation to Kathy, Tammy, and Tonya for their loving encouragement in this and every project I undertake.

Chapter One

A PROBLEM FACING CHURCHES TODAY

"The church is impoverished today because our sights are too low and our expertise underdeveloped for the development of adequate resources."

Raymond B. Knudsen[1]

Come with me as I visit three pastors.[2] First we will visit Bob Allen. Bob is senior pastor at Christ Church, a large suburban church in an affluent area. Christ Church is one of the largest churches in the denomination. When we arrive, Bob meets us at the door and graciously escorts us through the building. We are immediately struck by the beauty of the modern architecture and the religious artwork which graces the building. When we come to the sanctuary, Bob points out where recently it has been expanded to accommodate the overflowing crowds which attend each of the three Sunday morning services. Bob is highly regarded as a preacher, and people come from some distance each Sunday to hear him.

We conclude the tour, and Bob invites us to his office. He has been at Christ Church a good many years and he hopes to remain until he retires in a few more years. Obviously, he loves the people of this congregation deeply and he in turn is deeply loved by them. Bob says that he encounters only one major frustration in his ministry here. When we inquire what that is, he indicates that it is finances. "Last year we had a shortfall in our budget of over $100,000, and I am predicting a similar shortfall again this year."

I express surprise that the congregation would have such a shortfall in its operating budget. "There is absolutely no reason for it," Bob admits. "The congregation is capable of doing much more financially than it is currently doing. The fact of the matter is that I am very uncomfortable in talking with people about money. I wasn't trained to

1

do it; I don't know how to do it; and I'm not working with the key leadership in this area. In fact, I don't really know who the key financial leaders are."

The second pastor we visit is George Bidwell. George has been at Friendship Church for several years and has helped it grow from a small congregation into one of the most active and dynamic churches in the area. Many new homes are being built nearby, and young professional families are moving in. The church provides a ministry to them by offering daycare services in the educational wing. A number of these families have become active in the life of the church, attending worship and Bible study on a regular basis.

"Our greatest need," George says as he walks us through the church, "is for more space. We have simply outgrown our facilities. We don't have enough classrooms; our sanctuary is too small; and we cannot do the programming we want to do to continue to attract and involve the growing number of families in this area."

George went on to say that Friendship Church recently concluded a major capital campaign to address this situation. "We drew up some plans, shared them with the congregation, and invited their pledges. Because the need is so obvious, we were confident we would have no problem in raising the necessary dollars. We were sorely disappointed when less than half the needed amount was pledged. We have had to postpone some of our plans indefinitely."

In reflecting on the campaign, George noted that it was a new experience for the congregation and for him personally. "None of us had conducted a major campaign before. We thought that if we made the need known, people would respond accordingly. However, the largest commitments were not anywhere near what we had hoped for. Perhaps we did something wrong."

Our third visit is with Sarah Carson. Sarah is pastor of Community Church, a small congregation in a predominantly blue-collar community. Ten years ago the congregation built a new church, and she proudly shows us the facilities. As she does she explains how it has become a focal point for the community, with many community activities taking place in the building each week. In addition, the church sponsors a full range of activities and programs for its diverse membership of young and old.

An older member recently surprised the church. "She died and left the church with half a million dollars," Sarah explains. "We had no idea she had this kind of money or that she was planning to leave anything to the church. We were totally surprised and unprepared for this kind of gift."

Sarah went on to say that the gift has been a mixed blessing. "We haven't even received it yet, and already it is causing division within our church. A number of people think we should use it to pay off the debt on our mortgage. Others want to invest it and use only the earnings. I personally would like to see it used to expand our outreach ministries, but I am afraid many persons will want to use it to supplement our annual budget. Our current giving has already fallen off since the announcement of this gift was made."

Sarah wishes that a policy statement had been in place before this gift was received, outlining how bequests would be handled. "I think it will be very difficult now for us to agree amicably on the appropriate use of this money. I do not feel well prepared to offer leadership in this situation."

Bob Allen, George Bidwell, and Sarah Carson are highly competent pastors, performing important ministries in their respective settings. They are deeply loved and respected by their congregations. Another common thread running through their distinctive ministries, however, is the feeling of being ill prepared to provide leadership in matters dealing with money. For Bob this lack of preparation has meant a deficit in the annual budget; for George it has led to postponing needed expansion plans; and for Sarah it has resulted in conflict within the church over how to dispose of a planned gift.

Are their situations unique? Not at all! In visits with church leaders across the nation, I hear similar stories regularly. A common concern of clergy and laity alike is that many in church leadership positions are uncomfortable in providing financial leadership. Indeed, it often seems as though church leaders are less prepared to deal with money matters than almost any other aspect of their work.

Why is this so? Many pastors point out that they have not been trained in this area. Few seminaries offer courses in stewardship and fund raising, and few students feel the need for such courses—until their first financial campaign. Most ministerial students naively assume that "someone else" will take care of financial matters in the church. Fortunately, some seminaries are beginning to address this problem by offering courses on stewardship in the curriculum. Such courses focus on introducing students to a dynamic theology of stewardship and helping them develop practical fund raising methods based on this understanding. The fact remains, however, that whole generations of church leaders have had little or no training in this area.

Another reason for avoiding leadership in this area is based on the fear that talk of money will offend people. Many people are offended by the number of fund raising appeals today. A recent Gallup poll reported that nearly half of adult Americans believe there are too many fund raising appeals.[3] However, people want and need guidance in the area of stewardship and welcome talk about money which is open, honest, and based on ethical principles. Furthermore, if fund raising requests are handled appropriately, most people are not offended by being asked to support a worthy cause. Rather they are flattered to be invited, even if they cannot support the cause at the suggested level.

A third reason for avoiding leadership in fund raising is the low esteem in which such activity is held. A survey conducted in 1987 on behalf of the Conference on Funding the Christian Challenge found that nearly 40 percent of those polled felt that most Christian fund raising is neither ethical nor honest.[4] One can imagine that the widespread media coverage of fund misuse by televangelists in recent years has done little to change such attitudes.

Perhaps the reluctance of church leaders to provide decisive leadership in this area can best be summarized in one word: embarrassment. Many are embarrassed by their lack of knowledge and experience in fund raising. They are embarrassed at the prospect of discussing such a sensitive subject with influential people. And not insignificantly, they are embarrassed by the fund raising scandals of some well-publicized religious organizations.

Is it any wonder that church leaders would prefer to focus their attention elsewhere? Many do just that, hoping that the faithful will somehow enable the work of the church to continue. Sometimes this happens. More often than not, however, the refusal to deal decisively with stewardship issues has negative consequences.

One such consequence is that churches have not kept pace with the growing fund raising sophistication of other charitable organization. The competition for philanthropic dollars has become very intense, and many charitable organizations have developed such strategies as telemarketing, phonathons, videocassettes, and audiocassettes to tell their story and appeal for funds. In addition, many groups have hired professional fund raisers on a full-time or part-time basis and have relied on outside professional development counsel as well. Most churches, meanwhile, still tend to rely on the weekly offering and an annual pledge drive to meet their budgetary needs.

The result, not surprisingly, is that the percentage of income given to churches has decreased. According to a study released in 1988 by empty tomb, inc., individuals are giving a smaller percentage of their personal income to the church than they did in the past. From 1968 to 1985, while Americans' disposable after-tax income increased by 31 percent, the percentage of income given per member to church decreased 8.5 percent, the study concluded.[5] It appears that the old ways of doing things are no longer as effective and that church stewardship programs today must incorporate new fund raising insights.

The lack of financial leadership in our churches has produced an even more devastating consequence. Church members have not been helped to develop an appropriate theology of giving. As a result, many church people do not see their pattern of giving related in any meaningful way to their own spiritual growth. An essential part of the Christian message, however, proclaims that the two are intricately related. When this message is not taught boldly and with conviction, members often are not motivated to grow in their giving and an important part of their spiritual growth is stunted.

In today's society it is especially critical that Christians have a well-grounded understanding of the role giving plays in their own spiritual development. The competition for dollars comes not just from other charitable institutions, many of which perform important ministries and deserve to be supported; the intense competition for dollars comes also from our consumer-oriented society. Billions of dollars are spent annually seeking to persuade us that the key to happiness is found in having the right car, the right home, and the right clothes. The church must be equally bold in pointing out the flaws of such a trivial, self-centered philosophy and pointing toward a more excellent way to fulfillment.

At first glance the church appears to be doing all right in this task. After all, gifts to religious organizations far outweigh gifts to any other type of charity, accounting for nearly half of all charitable dollars. However, when one compares what American Protestants gave in 1985 to overseas missions ($1.3 billion) with what Americans spent that same year on lawns ($2 billion), cut flowers ($3.5 billion), and pets ($8 billion),[6] one quickly realizes that the Christian message is in danger of being drowned in a sea of self-satisfying affluence. People obviously are placing a higher value on their lifestyle than on their faith commitment.

This situation is not likely to change until church leaders take responsibility for making stewardship a top priority. Much more than meeting the church budget is at stake. The viability of our Christian witness, the opportunity for profound mission, and the ability to grow spiritually are all parts of taking stewardship seriously.

Although church leaders are called upon to fulfill many important roles, no role is more important than leadership in the area of stewardship. The church is impoverished today because we have not given adequate emphasis in the past to stewardship education and resource development. Leaders must now be willing to move beyond their embarrassment, timidity, and fear to gain expertise and comfortableness in the development of financial resources. Those who do will be well prepared to lead vital ministries in the years ahead.

The purpose of this book is to help church leaders begin to gain such expertise and comfortableness. The thesis of the book is that resource development is an essential part of ministry today and will become increasingly important in future decades.

Chapter 2 will develop a theological understanding of stewardship. Chapters 3 through 7 will focus on essential elements and strategies of fund raising which complement this theological understanding. Chapter 8 will suggest a timeline to implement a well-balanced program for the stewardship of financial resources.

TO SUMMARIZE

A problem facing many churches today is the lack of strong leadership in the area of stewardship, particularly the stewardship of financial resources. Church leaders—clergy and laity—have had little or no training in this area and they feel uncomfortable and embarrassed in encouraging financial support for the church's ministries.

Failure to provide decisive leadership in this area has had negative consequences for the church, including a decreasing percentage of charitable dollars directed toward churches, and a growing lack of understanding among church members of the relationship between giving and spiritual growth.

This book is written to assist church leaders in gaining necessary expertise in the stewardship of financial resources, so that persons will be invited to grow spiritually and the various ministries of the church will flourish.

Chapter Two

A THEOLOGY OF STEWARDSHIP

"If a Christian is serious about giving, it means living by a different set of values relating to money and its use than is common."

Douglas W. Johnson[1]

What motivates people to give? According to professional fund raisers, people give for many reasons. Robert F. Sharpe, for example, lists nine primary reasons: love, hate, fear, emulation, guilt, gratitude, response, tax deductions, and recognition.[2] To his list I would add one more: greed. Let's look at each of these.

Love. Giving is the foremost way of expressing love. When one feels genuine love, one is moved to give of oneself. Recognizing God's deep love toward them, Christians throughout the centuries have been moved to respond in kind by giving through the church.

The story is told of a pastor who made a plea for a special offering for some worthy cause. He watched as each member of the church laid a gift on the altar. After the service he singled out a young woman who was quite wealthy and told her he noticed she had given only a small amount. "Don't you love Jesus?" he asked. "Yes, I love him," she replied, "but I'm not crazy about him." When we are crazy about someone, when our love is genuine, our giving knows no bounds.

Hate. Just as love can be a powerful motivator, so can hate. A famous German poet is said to have left his estate to his wife on one condition—that she remarry. Then there would be at least one man to regret his death, the poet wrote. For people to use wills to express anger is not unusual. Charities have often been the recipients of bequests because parents have chosen to write out children who have disappointed them.

Fear. The fear of losing something of value prompts some persons to give. They may fear losing their crops, a sick child, or a job. Whatever the fear is, some persons believe that giving will appease God and help them avoid such a loss.

Emulation. Some give to imitate others. Especially if they have respect for another person, they may choose to support the same causes that the other supports. Or again, persons may emulate others, believing that it is "the thing to do" or "the cause" to support.

Guilt. Guilt is a major motivator. We've probably all heard the story of the person who wrote to the Internal Revenue Service saying: "Five years ago I did not pay all my taxes. Enclosed is a check for fifty dollars. If I still can't sleep, I'll send the other half." We can chuckle at the story, but at the same time we recognize that guilt is probably a motivator more often than we care to admit.

Gratitude. Recently a medical school received a multimillion dollar gift from a family. The gift was made out of gratitude for a family member's life being saved. Many gifts have been received by schools, churches, and other organizations by people grateful for something of value they have received from these organizations in the past.

Response. As simple as it sounds, people give because they are asked to make a gift. The flip side is also true. When persons are asked why they have never given to a specific organization in the past, the response is often, "No one ever asked me!"

Tax deductions. Tax deductions are seldom primary motivators for giving. They often help the already motivated person in deciding how and when to make a gift, however. Tax deductions also sometimes enable persons to make larger gifts than otherwise possible.

Recognition. Everyone appreciates recognition. Some people are motivated to give in order that their name, or values they hold dear, be preserved. Others give to honor the name of someone important to them. People often make gifts to memorialize a dear friend or a loved family member.

Greed. Believe it or not, greed is also a motivator. Some give because they believe that God prospers givers. Their giving is thus an investment which they hope will increase their own prosperity.

Love, of course, seems to be the purest motivator from the Christian standpoint. After all, our God is a God of love. Wouldn't it be grand if love motivated all of our giving? A Christian, of course, like any other person, is a complex human being and is often motivated by mixed emotions. When a Christian gives, he or she may be responding to one or more of the other motivators as well.

10

As Christian leaders we must ask ourselves, however, about how we encourage people to give. To which factors do we appeal? Are all the motivators appropriate for Christian fund raisers to use? As one looks at Christian fund raising today, one might well conclude that the answer is "yes." Indeed, some of the primary motivators used by prominent religious personalities are fear, greed, and guilt.

Take Oral Roberts, for example. In January 1987 he told his television viewers that he might die if they failed to donate $8 million for scholarships to the Oral Roberts University medical school. The fear tactic worked and the necessary funds were raised by the March 31 deadline.

The greed tactic worked equally well for Jim and Tammy Bakker for quite some time, enabling them to preach—and live—a lifestyle that offered physical well-being and financial gain. Only when news of a sex scandal and hush money broke in 1987 did viewers of PTL Ministries finally begin to question the extravagant lifestyle and gospel of greed promoted by the Bakkers.

Guilt has always been a popular way to solicit money. Many groups, including churches, still find it quite profitable to make people feel guilty for being born in a land of plenty.

Fortunately, some people choose not to be associated with such negative tactics, recognizing that they are a repudiation of much of what Christianity stands for. Roberts was soundly criticized by both the religious and secular communitites for his appeal to fear; some believe the appeal may have permanently damaged his ministry. At the very least, his tactic heightened attention to the inappropriateness of fear in religious fund raising.

Though the PTL Ministries of Jim and Tammy Bakker have come to an end, other forms of the prosperity gospel undoubtedly will spring up to take PTL's place. When these other forms are presented, one can hope that persons will recognize that giving in the hope of prospering "is not giving but trading. It is not being generous. It is striking a good bargain. It is not risking anything. It is taking out good social insurance with the Celestial Casualty Company." [3]

Similarly, one can hope that more Christians will begin to see the irony of church appeals based on guilt. "It probably is one of the ironies of all time that the church—the one community which has been called into existence to proclaim the dissolution of guilt as humanity's

11

most anxious burden—is in the business of seeking money by deliberately provoking people to feel guilty."[4]

Unfortunately, whatever works in fund raising often has become acceptable. As church leaders we should point to a more excellent way, insisting on fund raising standards and practices which are consistent with Christian values and beliefs. What is needed is a solid theology of stewardship, based on the highest Judeo-Christian principles, which can guide our fund raising activities.

The Bible is a rich repository for developing a theology of stewardship. In fact, it provides an almost inexhaustible supply of information, reminding one that stewardship is not a side issue, but a central part of the faith.

In the very first chapter of Genesis, God appoints man and woman as stewards over the fish of the sea, the birds of the air, and every living thing that moves upon the earth (Gen. 1:28). Some have interpreted this dominion over the rest of the earth as a license to plunder, pollute, and destroy the earth, but this is a terrible misinterpretation of the scripture. The Psalms remind us that "the earth is the LORD's and the fulness thereof, the world and those who dwell therein" (24:1). All the resources of the world belong to God. Our responsibility as stewards is to care for these resources that have been entrusted to us in the same manner that God would. We learn that God's manner is compassionate; God seeks to give food to all in due season and to satisfy "the desire of every living thing" (145:16).

The Book of Job paints a portrait of the good steward as one who is also compassionate, delivering the poor, helping the fatherless, and bringing joy to the widow, eyes to the blind, feet to the lame, and justice to the victims of injustice (Job 29-31). The book is also a solemn reminder to the preachers of prosperity that being a good steward does not ensure protection against disaster and calamity.

The Old Testament prophets also build upon the theme that God calls us to act compassionately toward all of creation, particularly the poor. Isaiah reminds us that God calls us to feed the hungry, shelter the homeless, and clothe the naked (Isa. 58:7). Micah condemns covetousness, which victimizes the poor (Mic. 2:2). Amos has harsh words for those who live lives of luxury while ignoring the needy, and calls for justice to "roll down like waters, and righteousness like an everflowing stream" (Amos 5:24).

Nowhere in the Old Testament is the effect of God's ownership of all

12

things more clearly delineated than in Leviticus, Numbers, and Deuteronomy, where the well-known tithing legislation is described (Lev. 27:30-32; Num. 18:20-32; Deut. 14:22-29). In addition, one finds in Leviticus a description of the Year of Jubilee, which was to arrange for land reform on a regular basis, so no one would be permanently poor. The principle of the tithe and jubilee was important because it ensured that a portion of what was rightfully God's was returned to help care for the poor and needy.

In the New Testament, the Book of Acts provides a glimpse of stewardship practices in the early church. Members shared all things in common, selling their individual possessions and distributing to those in need (Acts 2:44,45). This method of giving apparently was successful, as "there was not a needy person among them" (Acts 4:34).

God's spirit of compassion is again evoked in the epistles. In James we read: "If a brother or sister is ill-clad and in lack of daily food, and one of you says to them, 'Go in peace, be warmed and filled,' without giving them the things needed for the body, what does it profit? So faith by itself, if it has no works, is dead" (James 2:15-17). In the first letter of John we are confronted with the compelling question, "But if any one has the world's goods and sees his brother in need, yet closes his heart against him, how does God's love abide in him?" (1 John 3:17). In the first letter of Peter, we are reminded, "As each has received a gift, employ it for one another, as good stewards of God's varied grace" (1 Peter 4:10). Words directed specifically to the rich in this world remind them "to do good, to be rich in good deeds, liberal and generous . . . so that they may take hold of the life which is life indeed" (1 Tim. 6:18,19).

The Apostle Paul devoted considerable attention to matters of stewardship. In 2 Corinthians 8 and 9, he praised the Macedonian churches for their generosity in the midst of poverty and challenged the church at Corinth to be equally generous, reminding them that "God loves a cheerful giver" (2 Cor. 9:7). He emphasized that all we have is a gift from God (1 Cor. 4:7) and is to be liberally and cheerfully shared (Rom. 12:8). He added a new dimension to the understanding of stewardship when he proclaimed that giving without love means nothing (1 Cor. 13:3).

Jesus, of course, was the greatest stewardship teacher of all. He said more about money than about any other subject, including prayer. In the Gospels, one verse in six focuses on material possessions, and

13

these verses are punctuated with such memorable sayings as "Where your treasure is, there will your heart be also" (Matt. 6:21); "Render to Caesar the things that are Caesar's, and to God the things that are God's" (Mark 12:17); "Every one to whom much is given . . . will much be required" (Luke 12:48); and "God so loved the world that he gave his only Son" (John 3:16).

Through the parables Jesus expanded the limits of stewardship beyond previous understandings. Through metaphor and story he taught that stewardship is a way of life which permeates all aspects of our being—our attitudes as well as our actions, our desires as well as our deeds. In no less than fifteen parables, he taught what it means to be a responsible steward: two forgiven debtors (Luke 7:41-43); the good Samaritan (Luke 10:29-37); the rich fool (Luke 12:16-21); the faithful and wise steward (Luke 12:42-48); the fruitless fig tree (Luke 13:6-9); the unjust steward (Luke 16:1-9); the rich man and Lazarus (Luke 16:19-31); the pounds (Luke 19:11-27); the treasure hidden in a field (Matt. 13:44); the pearl of great price (Matt. 13:45-46); the unforgiving servant (Matt. 18:23-35); the laborers in the vineyard (Matt. 20:1-16); the wise and foolish maidens (Matt. 25:1-13); the talents (Matt. 25:14-30); and the judgment scene (Matt. 25:31-46).

Two other sayings of Jesus have special relevance to our understanding of responsible stewardship. The first is his response to the rich young ruler who asked what he needed to do to inherit eternal life. He seemed to anticipate some religious or spiritual formula as a response. Instead, Jesus pointed to the world's needs and declared that only by helping to meet them could the young man's own need for eternal life be met. "You lack one thing; go, sell what you have, and give to the poor, and you will have treasure in heaven; and come, follow me" (Mark 10:21). To give liberally from one's possessions is a final and necessary step for one's own spiritual growth. The man was not prepared for such a statement; neither are many others who seek to follow Jesus even today.

The second saying of Jesus that has relevance in this context is his paradoxical statement, "Whoever would save his life will lose it; and whoever loses his life for my sake and the gospel's will save it" (Mark 8:35). Perhaps there is no better summary of the good steward than this. The steward is not someone intent on preserving his or her own life. Rather, the steward is one who invests oneself in things beyond self—in the causes of Christ—and who in the process discovers life at its deepest, richest level.

In summary, the Bible offers the following insights into our understanding of stewardship:

- God is the source of all of life. We have been given resources to use, but not to own.
- Stewardship is a way of life in which we seek to manage well all that has been entrusted to us—time, talent, and treasure—and to use these gifts compassionately for the benefit of all God's creation.
- Jesus epitomized the good steward. He owned no possessions and gave himself in complete service to God. Through his life he demonstrated that stewardship is an outward and visible sign of an inward commitment to God.
- Responding to opportunities to serve others compassionately leads to one's own spiritual growth and true fulfillment.

From the prominent role stewardship plays in the Bible, one can readily conclude that the church today cannot ignore this issue. Talking about how to use what God has given us is holy talk, deeply theological and an essential part of our ministry.

The question, of course, becomes how may we best engage in such talk? How do we as church leaders effectively apply the biblical understanding of stewardship to the world in which we live today?

We can begin by affirming that the mission of the church today is essentially one of stewardship. Some years ago H. Richard Niebuhr succinctly defined the purpose of the church as "the increase of the love of God and neighbor." [5] More recently Douglas W. Johnson defined a steward as one who "uses whatever he or she has and possesses to the glory of God and helps make life better for others." [6] How well these two definitions complement one another and point to the truth that the church as a corporate body should model stewardship (glorifying God and making life better for others) and should encourage its individual members to grow in their stewardship commitment (loving God and neighbor in demonstrable ways in their daily lives).

Second, we can teach that stewardship has to do with all of one's life, not just one's financial resources. One author suggests, "Perhaps if we took a long hard look at how to teach people to manage time, their homes and resources as well as their funds, we might see incomes rise, families stick together, and fewer social problems."[7] Whether or not all these positive changes would take place, the author makes a valid point in suggesting that churches must find ways to teach people how to be stewards of all resources.

Third, we can stress that just as important as the church's need to receive in order to carry out its mission is our need to give for our own spiritual development. We need to invest ourselves in things beyond ourselves—in programs and projects and people that will outlast our own lives—if we are to become fulfilled human beings. Joe W. Walker suggests that real growth in giving comes only as the church shares with people "a motivation based on their need to give instead of just telling them about the church's need to receive."[8] Such an approach to stewardship would be radically new for many churches. Merely contemplating the growth that could take place if churches would institute this approach is exciting. The growth would not be only in dollars for missions, but spiritual growth and changed lives in those who caught a new vision of giving.

Fourth, we can lift up giving as an opportunity. Giving is an opportunity to live out the gospel in daily life by serving God and others. It is an opportunity to express our love to God by helping others. Giving is an opportunity to preach, teach, heal, evangelize, and reconcile in the name of Jesus. It is an opportunity to make God's love known throughout the world by supporting physicians, evangelists, teachers, agricultural experts, radio technicians, nurses, pilots, and others who serve as Christ's witnesses in lands near and far.

Giving is also an opportunity to discover personal joy and satisfaction which far exceeds the short-lived pleasures promoted by society. Through giving we invest ourselves in programs and projects around the world which expand our personal horizons. Knowing that we are making a critical difference in the lives of others brings a sense of fulfillment and completeness that cannot be duplicated in any other manner. In losing ourselves in projects bigger than ourselves, we find life. As church leaders we will be far ahead in our efforts to teach stewardship if we lift up giving as an opportunity rather than an institutional necessity.

Fifth, we can help people evaluate their priorities and life patterns against the biblical standard of stewardship. What does it mean to lose one's life in today's world? In our affluent society, is tithing an appropriate response to God's gracious gifts, or is it a starting point for even greater involvement? We can encourage members to analyze how they use all their resources and to see the use of these gifts as symbols of their values and priorities. For example, what percentage of time is spent at work, at play, with family, and in helping others? What talents are being used to enrich the world outside one's work? What does our checkbook say about our values? For most of us, there is probably no more succinct a theological statement than that document!

In areas where persons fail to meet the biblical standard of stewardship—and most of us will find such areas in our lives—we as church leaders can invite growth in love of God and neighbor. Some will choose not to grow, as did the rich young ruler, finding the invitation too costly. However, we can offer nothing less, for our invitation is simply the Christian invitation for new life—new life for others through our gifts and for ourselves through our giving.

Extending an invitation to grow in stewardship commitment presents two challenges. First is the challenge of how to present the invitation. The method of invitation must be consistent with the message. We are offering joy, satisfaction, fulfillment, love, wholeness, and spiritual growth. There is no room for fear, greed, or guilt. Neither is there room for coercion or manipulation. The invitation must be freely extended and just as freely rejected if one so chooses. Jesus did not coerce the rich young ruler to accept his invitation, but let him walk away from it when he decided he was not prepared to pay the price.

A second challenge is how to encourage people to consider seriously the invitation. The invitation is radically different from society's understanding of happiness and well-being. Accepting it will mean living by a different set of values than is common today. How do we positively encourage people to move beyond an unthinking acquiescence to society's values regarding money and possessions so they can discover for themselves a joy society can never offer? Finding the answer to this question is undoubtedly one of the most difficult tasks facing the church.

The answer lies somewhere in the vision the church presents to its members. Daniel H. Burnham, well-known architect and city planner, remarked in 1907, "Make no little plans; they have no magic to stir men's blood and probably themselves will not be realized. Make big plans; aim high in hope and work."[9] The church might well take his words to heart as it seeks to create an invitation which is attractive and compelling. The church's vision and plan for the future must be big enough and bold enough to capture people's attention, their imagination, and their commitment.

A tall order? Certainly. A great opportunity? Yes. A task force for the timid? No. But as church leaders we can move beyond our timidity and fears and embarrassment, knowing that we offer opportunities big enough to change lives.

The payoff for church leaders is that in extending the invitation for persons to grow in their stewardship commitment, leaders can themselves receive immense satisfaction. For as they bring together the needs of the church (to be a channel for mission) and the needs of individuals (to find fulfillment in something greater than themselves), they have the opportunity to witness the gospel coming alive!

Perhaps an appropriate way to conclude this chapter is to share my own personal journey as a church leader, a journey from reluctant fund raiser to staunch believer in fund raising as a ministry. My purpose in sharing this journey is to invite other church leaders to move beyond their reluctance and join me in the excitement of this calling.

I began my professional ministry as a local church pastor. During those years as pastor, I regarded fund raising as a necessary imposition in order to meet the church budget and pay the bills. The budget was met each year, and some extra fund raising activities were even held, such as a pension drive one year. However, these were regarded merely as diversions from "real ministry" which included preaching, pastoral care, and teaching. The satisfactions of local church ministry came from working with people on the cutting edges of their lives—marriage, birth, death—and helping them find some meaning in their life journeys.

From there I became campus minister and taught religion at a church-related university. Once again the satisfaction was working with people as they made major decisions regarding career, spouse, and values. Teaching continued to be a rewarding way to help people broaden their horizons.

Then one day I was challenged to broaden my own horizons. The president of the university invited me to head up the fund raising office. I knew what the satisfactions of local church ministry were. I knew what the satisfactions of campus ministry and teaching were. But

I could not imagine what the satisfactions of fund raising would be. With some reluctance I finally accepted the offer.

My experience at the college was several years ago. I now am serving in the development office of a seminary. Obviously I have found some satisfactions in fund raising. Again, the relationships with people have brought me the greatest satisfactions. What a joy to be in partnership with such a diverse group of people who are interested in making a positive difference in the world. Let me introduce you to a few of them.

Edna is a woman who is in her eighties. She lives very modestly in her three-room apartment. She spends her days visiting shut-ins, making hospital calls, and delivering church newsletters. She disciplines herself to live on pennies so that she can give the rest away. One year she even gave up drinking coffee so that she would have a bit more to give to a hunger project about which she cares deeply. Depressing? Not at all. I have never met a person more excited about life. She began chasing butterflies in her seventies, and today she is an expert on monarch butterflies. She talks enthusiastically about how she raises them, tags them, and researches them. She concluded one of our visits by remarking how much God has taught her about life through butterflies. As I left her modest abode, I thought to myself how much God had taught me about life through her.

Alice is a woman who lives on the other end of the financial spectrum. On various occasions she has shared with me some of the burden she feels in being wealthy and her desire not to become trapped by her wealth. The Word becomes flesh in her as she tells me that her satisfactions in life come not in her personal creature comforts, but in giving herself to things beyond herself. Her eyes light up as she talks about a mission project she supports in Kansas City, about a young student from another country she is helping to educate, about a school for the retarded in which she has an interest, and about a Bible translation project that brings her much satisfaction. Her horizons broaden my own.

Lloyd is a successful attorney. His life has been changed as he has worked on the tax forms of some clients. As he prepared their taxes and saw their level of commitment to various causes, he was moved to assess his own values and commitments. As a result, his life has taken on a new direction.

I wish you could also meet Fern and Bob and Fran and Phil—and the list goes on. The reason these relationships are so satisfying is because I have grown so much from them. The gospel has come alive for me as I have seen these people measure their lives against the biblical standard and grow in their stewardship commitment. Through my relationships with them, I have come to a much deeper understanding of what it means to find one's life by losing it. These people are some of the most vitally alive Christians I know.

The fact is that I have come to see fund raising not simply as a satisfying career, but as a vitally important ministry. This ministry provides adequate financial undergirding for critically important work. Some suggest that lack of funding is the major impediment to eradicating hunger, developing self-help programs, and spreading the gospel of Jesus Christ. What could be more rewarding than to enable ministries of relief, development, and proclamation to be carried out in Christ's name?

A ministry of fund raising also can encourage spiritual growth. I have had the rare opportunity to see lives take on new meaning as people devote themselves to causes greater than themselves. Through my work I have come firmly to believe that giving is one of the most important elements in aiding a person's spiritual growth. As people invest themselves and their resources in causes which demand their all, the gods of society lose their hold and the fruits of the Spirit begin to grow.

TO SUMMARIZE

People give for many reasons, but church leaders should seek to motivate giving based on a solid theology of Christian stewardship. Such a theology recognizes that God is the source of all gifts. Jesus, the good steward, invites persons to use these gifts in a manner which benefits all creation and demonstrates a commitment to God.

Thus, an important mission of the church is to invite persons to a life of stewardship. Such a lifestyle glorifies God, makes the world better for others, and nurtures a person's own spiritual development. Presenting the invitation to a life of stewardship offers the following two challenges: how can we make it attractive enough and how can we make it compelling enough to be given serious consideration. Church leaders can have no greater priority than addressing these challenges.

Chapter Three

ESSENTIAL ELEMENTS OF FUND RAISING

"To show great love for God and our neighbor we need not do great things. It is how much love we put in the doing that makes our offering Something Beautiful for God."

Mother Teresa of Calcutta[1]

In the last chapter I noted that stewardship involves living one's whole life in grateful response to God's love for us. "We love, because he first loved us" (1 John 4:19). Love is the key motivating factor which shapes how a Christian steward spends time, talents, and treasure.

In this and remaining chapters, the focus of attention will be on stewardship of treasure, or financial resources. The purpose is not to negate the importance of stewardship in the rest of one's life, but simply to put some necessary parameters on the scope of this book. In focusing on stewardship of treasure, I hope that church leaders will be assisted in developing congregations that are spiritually alive and financially supportive of the church's mission. I also encourage church leaders to avail themselves of other resources to assist their congregations in developing their stewardship of time and talent.

Two major challenges face church leaders who seek to invite persons to grow in the stewardship of financial resources: presenting the invitation in a positive manner and making the invitation compelling enough to be given serious consideration. This chapter will address the first challenge. Chapter 4 will focus on the latter.

Mother Teresa's words at the beginning of this chapter highlight an important truth: The most essential element in making gifts is the attitude with which they are made. That attitude, for Christians, should be one of love—a love which is created and energized by God's love and which leads to a spontaneous overflow of giving. Such an attitude

23

sees giving as an opportunity to be in partnership with Christ in fulfilling God's purposes in the world.

Obviously such a loving attitude does not just happen. Many fund raisers begin with the assumption that people give out of self-interest; these fund raisers develop their fund raising strategies accordingly. However, if our faith and heritage suggest that love is the primary attitude underlying Christian giving, then it behooves church leaders to find ways to nurture this attitude and to foster compassion and care as primary motivators rather than relying solely on self-interest.

One way to nurture the attitude of love is to make sure this essential element permeates all invitations to give. In other words, church leaders themselves should model attitudes of love and compassion in all they do and say. Realistically, however, one must recognize that such an attitude is often developed only over a period of time through prayer, study, and actual practice in giving. Thus, church leaders should find ways to promote an ongoing program of stewardship education in the church which includes all of these dimensions. More is written about this in Chapter 5.

T. A. Kantonen undoubtedly is correct when he writes that the true beginning of Christian stewardship takes place "through complete self-surrender to the love of God in Christ."[2] Giving then becomes the living expression of one's faith and is not bound by legalism, guilt, or duty. Rather, giving is an opportunity to respond, freely and joyfully, to one's wholehearted commitment to Christ. Thus, evangelism and stewardship go hand in hand, and church leaders should welcome programs of discipleship as opportunities to enhance stewardship and vice versa.

Besides bearing witness to the power of Christ's love in their own lives, church leaders involved in talking with others about money will be well equipped for their task if they also demonstrate the following qualities:

Honesty. Not surprisingly, when persons are asked which qualities are important to them in deciding whether or not to begin supporting an organization, the quality considered most important is honesty. People expect and deserve openness and honesty from any charitable organization about how their gifts will be used. Although this honesty seems basic, it must be remembered that only half of the people queried in a recent survey thought fund raising by Christian churches and organizations was honest and ethical. Church leaders must do a

24

better job of taking the initiative to inform members where the gifts are going and what they are accomplishing. Likewise, they should welcome inquiries and should seek to respond to such questions as forthrightly as possible.

Compassion. Another quality considered very important by prospective givers is whether or not an organization is perceived to be caring and compassionate. Is the organization involved in some significant ministries of caring which are helping to alleviate some of the crying needs of the world? Donors want to make sure their dollars are going where they will make a difference, where they will help to address some important need. Persons respond generously to disaster appeals because the needs of others are so obvious, and organizations are responding with compassion. Church leaders who can demonstrate care and compassion in their own manner and who can point to the caring qualities of their church's ministries will develop confident supporters.

Care. Just as important as the organization's compassion for others is its care for the individual donor. Does the church really care about the individual as a person and not just a donor? How is such care demonstrated? Those who talk to others about money must continually remember that all persons are children of God and are important for who they are and not just for the resources they have. The church that demonstrates care for each person and communicates that the giver is always more important than the gift will again take a major step toward developing long-term supporters. Such care can be demonstrated in a variety of ways, including getting to know persons as individuals, encouraging their involvement beyond their financial support, and making sure they are visited at times other than when gifts are requested.

Integrity. The integrity of the leadership will set the tone for any organization. Leaders who talk to others about money become, for many people, the organization they represent. Thus, the personal qualities of the leaders, as well as the qualities of the organization, are significant to the prospective donor. The leaders should have personal high standards of honesty and compassion and should demonstrate consistency in their personal and professional lives. It should be obvious to the prospective donor that it is not greed, but genuine need, which motivates any request for support. Leaders with integrity will be motivated to seek financial support because of a genuine commitment to the cause they represent, and they will have demonstrated that commitment by their own generous support.

Accountability. In recent years the church has been rocked with scandals of flagrant and intentional misuse of funds. For every well-publicized scandal there are other horror stories about how churches have unintentionally misused funds through poor management or lack of appropriate fiscal controls. It is unfortunately true that what would be regarded as poor practice in the business world is often commonplace in religious organizations. And yet, the gospel of Jesus Christ should make churches more, not less, accountable, for they have a moral as well as a legal obligation to their people. At the very least, accountability requires that all interested persons have the right to know where an organization's support comes from and where the dollars go. Accountability also demands that churches follow a standard set of accounting guidelines, institute appropriate audit procedures, and adhere to a written code of fund raising ethics. Only those organizations that show appropriate accountability have a right to request support. No one should feel obligated to subsidize bad management.

Vision. Few people are motivated to make significant gifts simply to maintain an organization. They need a vision which catches their eye, stirs their soul, and challenges their pocketbook. The church leaders are responsible for creating such a vision—showing what is possible if donor and recipient come together in partnership to address major concerns. In testing the idea for a major statewide church campaign recently, 81 percent of the laity and 86 percent of the clergy indicated they would give less than $1,000 over a three-year period. According to a campaign committee member, those figures represented not a lack of ability but a lack of having been challenged. One can surmise that a majority of those who continue to give a dollar a week in the collection plate have likewise failed to be challenged by a vision which suggests more than "business as usual."

Communication skills. Having developed a vision for the church, next comes the task of articulating this vision in a way that people will want to respond as generously as possible. Most people are not inspired by facts and figures as much as they are by stories. Thus, imagination and creativity are required to translate budget projections into concrete pictures of how needs will be met and lives changed. Communicating the vision cannot be scripted; it must be a dialogue between those telling the story and those hearing it, with the teller sharing from the heart why this is important, but also listening with the heart to the questions and concerns of the hearer. Through this mutual give-and-take emerges the possibility that the hearer will want to become a partner in this cause.

Optimism. Someone once suggested that fund raising is a series of disappointments, interspersed with a few happy surprises. Although this summary is hardly an accurate portrayal of the fund raising process, it does suggest that a healthy dose of optimism is a most welcome quality. A number of people—sometimes it seems a majority—will fail to respond in spite of a brilliant articulation of a compelling vision presented as honestly and compassionately as possible. The optimist recognizes this reception as a fact of life and continues to tell the story, confident that all will work out well. Such confidence seems especially appropriate for those "telling the stories of Jesus," for these stories have stood the test of time and have inspired persons throughout the ages.

Enthusiasm. If church leaders believe deeply in the causes they are presenting, these leaders will find it easy to speak about the causes with some enthusiasm. Such enthusiasm is important because persons are motivated by emotion as much as they are by reason. Enthusiasm is a contagious emotion, and often persons find themselves getting excited about a cause when they see the sparkle in the eye and hear the fervor in the voice of a presenter. Such enthusiasm cannot be faked, but must come from the heart. This honesty of emotion is another reason why one must make one's own financial commitment to a cause before inviting others to do so. Having made a financial commitment increases enthusiasm and opens the door to the possibility of sharing with others what one has done. Little carries more weight in fund raising than an enthusiastic personal testimony.

Sensitivity. Sensitivity to each individual's personal situation is critically important. Oftentimes leaders will identify those who they believe could be the major contributors to a cause, only to discover in talking with these persons that personal circumstances may prevent major support at that time. Perhaps the potential contributors have made a major pledge commitment to another charity; perhaps they have incurred significant medical expense; or perhaps they are having to provide financial assistance to a family member. Whatever the reason, church leaders would do well to honor such circumstances rather than push hard for a commitment. Certainly they should "tell the story" and assess the level of interest. They should even explore together alternative ways of involvement if the interest is there. The church is more likely to win respect and long-term support, however, if it is sensitive to short-term circumstances.

Listening Skills. The best way to learn about individual circumstances is to listen. Church leaders need to tell their story as persuasively as possible. They also need to listen as intently as possible. In fact, most professional fund raisers probably would agree that in any fund raising call, the majority of time should be spent in listening. People rarely have an opportunity to talk about themselves, and when invited to do so, they usually respond with gusto. The astute listener can learn about a person's interests, hobbies, and family situation. Much can be learned about what brings a person greatest satisfaction. This information can be enormously helpful in making requests for financial support which meet the church's goals at the same time that they meet an individual's plans and dreams.

Patience. In a very real sense, seeking funds is much like farming. Seeds are planted and nurtured with the hope of being harvested. The parable of the sower is good to recall in fund raising; some seeds will fall on rocky soil, some among thorns, and some on good soil. However, even those seeds which fall on good soil may take a long while before they are harvested. As in other areas of ministry, church leaders who plant ideas for financial support may not be the ones to harvest them. These seeds require cultivation. Sometimes the cultivation process is relatively brief; other times years may elapse before the process comes to fruition and a major gift is received. Thus, patience, perseverance, and faithfulness in planting seeds are all necessary.

Discussion in the last few pages has centered on the qualities needed to present positively the invitation to grow in stewardship of financial resources. Is developing these qualities all there is to cultivating stewardship? Many church leaders still believe that seeking financial resources requires slick, high-pressure presentations from salespersons with special skills enabling them to push for gifts until donors succumb.

Nothing could be further from the truth. In fact, most professional fund raisers undoubtedly would agree that the above list contains the most important qualities to look for in a fund raiser. There are, of course, basic fund raising strategies to learn. These can be easily learned, however, if the appropriate attitude and personal qualities are there. If they are not, no fund raising strategy will be effective for long.

Interestingly, although church leaders do not normally see themselves as fund raisers, many of them possess to a high degree the qualities needed to be successful in fund raising. After all, the qualities that brought them to leadership within the church are the same qualities necessary for successful fund raising. Good fund raising is not dependent upon aggressive, high-pressure, or manipulative techniques. Rather, it is based upon developing lifelong relationships between individuals and the organization, relationships of mutual respect and partnership.

Therefore, it is not surprising that a good percentage of professional fund raisers today have backgrounds in church leadership. Most fund raisers come into fund raising through some other profession. The high number coming from church leadership positions attests to the attractive personal and professional qualities that church people can bring to fund raising. Church leaders can be very effective fund raisers if they are willing to learn some of the basics.

Let's turn then to some of the basics. As was noted earlier, developing financial support is a cultivation process. G. T. Smith, president emeritus of Chapman College, suggests the following process, or cycle, which involves five steps, all beginning with the letter "I".[3]

1. Identification
2. Information
3. Interest
4. Involvement
5. Investment

A closer look at each of these steps is warranted.

1. *Identification.* The first step in any fund raising effort is to identify those who could be potential supporters and, further, to identify those who could provide leadership gift support. How are such people identified? Potential supporters would include all current donors, all current members who are not donors (which one hopes would be few in number), those who attend church but are not members, past members who maintain an interest in the church, those who grew up in the church, and others suggested from any of these groups.

29

In other words, potential supporters include persons who have a past, present, or potential affiliation with the church.

From this rather broad list of potential supporters will be found a smaller list of those who can provide leadership gift support. How are they identified? Often these leaders are the people who are demonstrating their interest on a regular basis through sharing their time and talent in the church. They may be serving on committees and boards, teaching classes, or singing in the choir. In a dozen different ways, potential leaders proclaim their commitment to the church. The leadership gift support generally will come from these people who are involved most closely in the life of the church.

Another important way to identify leadership gift support is to look at the giving history of church members. Two assumptions sometimes prevent the church leadership from doing this.

First, leaders sometimes assume that those who have given generously in the past should not be considered, for they have done what they can do. Experience has shown that this assumption is false. People do not give away all their resources, and past supporters tend to be the best prospects for future support. Just as it should not be assumed that past supporters will continue giving at a similar level, it is equally inappropriate to assume that they cannot. People rarely make their largest gift when they begin supporting an organization. The likelihood is great that as their involvement and interest grow, so will their gifts, culminating perhaps in a lifetime gift which includes their estate plans.

Second, some clergy believe that knowing the giving histories of parishioners is inappropriate. These persons believe that having this information might affect how they relate to church members. Such an attitude seems naive at best and disastrous at worst. Can you imagine a corporate CEO saying it is not important to know where the money is coming from or a businessperson saying it really is not necessary to know which customers are in arrears in their payments? Is it any more appropriate for church leaders to take a cavalier approach regarding the source of their support?

Besides helping to identify the best prospects for leadership gift support in the future, assessing the giving pattern of parishioners on a regular basis is also one of the best ways to take the spiritual pulse of church members. In one church the pastor asks to be informed immediately if a parishioner stops or lowers giving. The pastor believes this warrants a personal visit to determine if there is a personal crisis, a drifting away from the church, or some dissatisfaction. The pastor has learned that this approach is far superior to the typical one of waiting until it is too late to respond effectively to personal or spiritual need. Rather than hindering one's ministry, this pastor believes that information about giving patterns makes for more effective ministry.

Certainly, church leaders need to be discreet with the knowledge they have about other people's giving, and the number of leaders who have such information should be tightly limited. The top leadership, however, has the right, indeed the obligation, to have and use this information for the good of the whole church.

Why do leadership gift supporters need to be identified? Why not just include everyone in fund raising appeals? Everyone should be invited to participate at some point in fund raising efforts, but leadership givers will set the pace and will determine the success or failure of any effort. Traditional figures suggest that 80 percent of a fund raising goal will come from 20 percent of the donors. In actuality, the figures are even more dramatic than that. "National gift patterns indicate that 90 percent of the money in well-organized development programs will tend to come from 5 percent of the donors, dramatizing the value of large gift solicitation."[4] Clearly, identifying those who can assist in making a fund raising effort successful is important.

Identification, then, is an important first step which sets the stage for any successful fund raising effort. This step provides church leaders with an overview of who the potential supporters are and also indicates who might be able to provide leadership gift support.

2. *Information.* Information is a two-way street. It involves gathering information about the potential donor and sharing the information with the potential donor about the fund raising effort.

Questions of ethics recently have arisen in the fund raising world about what are appropriate ways to gather information on prospective donors. Traditionally, organizations have relied on information gathered from such sources as probate, tax, corporate, and social club records; newspaper articles; and talks with prospects' friends. Some donors have been outraged to learn that organizations have gathered information about them and their resources in this manner.

One way to avoid such anger and dispel any questions about the ethical propriety of gathering information is to learn about potential donors from the potential donors themselves. Actually, such open research is superior to surreptitious research in several respects. First, the information provided will be up-to-date, whereas information gathered by other means may well not be. Second, the information can be put in appropriate context ("Yes, we have a good income. We also have four children in college and two elderly parents we are helping to support."). Third, the "researcher" comes to know a whole person with individual tastes, values, and interests, rather than just a potential donor. Fourth, a personal visit allows the potential donor the opportunity to become acquainted or better acquainted with someone from the organization, thus personalizing the organization for that person.

A number of fund raisers have found this personal research method to be a very satisfactory way to learn more about potential donors. I use this method almost exclusively and believe that more helpful information can be learned in a half-hour visit than in hours of research at the county courthouse or library. This methodology seems to lend itself especially well to religious organizations since they have a tradition of pastoral calling on members and are concerned about the whole person and about building and maintaining relationships. A visit to a family's home can be a great way to be brought up-to-date on personal situations within the family and to share information about the church.

Sharing information about the church is the second half of the equation, and how this information is shared is critically important. James Gregory Lord correctly observes that talking about an organization's needs is ineffective. It is far more effective to talk about the opportunities that an organization offers donors to invest in solutions.[5] Church leaders should be poised to show persons that through the church they have one of the finest opportunities available to invest in solutions to human and societal needs. Few other organizations will invest donors' resources as efficiently or effectively and give them the satisfaction of knowing they are making a significant difference in the world.

Consider these facts. The federal government needs three dollars to administer one dollar's worth of foreign aid. Private agencies can administer the same dollar with less effort, between twenty-seven and forty-two cents. And the church? The church does it for less than eight cents! The point is that church leaders must be convinced they are offering potential donors a significant opportunity. If they are not convinced themselves, it will be apparent to others. If they are, their enthusiasm will be contagious.

Information is thus an important second step in the cultivation cycle because it allows the prospective donor and the organization to learn more about one another and their respective goals.

3. *Interest.* Successful organizations offer donors opportunities not only to meet the needs of others, but also to find personal fulfillment at the same time. Giving, whether it be of time, talent, or treasure, should provide opportunities for donors to pursue an interest, fulfill a dream, or leave a mark in the world.

The third step in the cultivation cycle is thus to find out what a person's interests are and to further those interests within the life of the church. Once again, one of the best ways to learn about those interests is through the personal visit. A visit to one's home affords a great opportunity to note hobbies, special skills, interests, and activities. A visit to share information about the church can be easily expanded to include this step of learning about the personal interests of church members.

Another way to learn about individual interests is through a "time and talent" survey. One church effectively uses such a survey by asking each new member to fill one out upon joining the church. The survey is personalized for that local church and lists dozens of different ways that persons can be involved, from entering data on the church's computer to serving on the finance committee, from making banners for worship to preparing meals for the hungry, from providing rides for shut-ins to serving as ushers on Sunday morning. Literally every opportunity for involvement in and beyond the church is listed.

Once these surveys are filled out, they are permanently filed in the church office. Information is sent to the appropriate leaders regarding areas of interest. These surveys provide helpful information for the nominating committee each year and provide a continual list of potential leaders for various projects and programs. A distinguishing feature of this church is how it uses the survey to involve new members early on. Each new member is invited to become involved in the life of the church in an area of his or her interest within the first month of joining.

The third step in the cultivation process is the creative task of matching the interests of the individual with the goals of the organization, thus leading to meaningful involvement.

4. *Involvement.* Are you interested in children? How about teaching a class? or coordinating a tutoring program? or serving on the daycare center board? or assisting with the children's choir?

Are you interested in missions? How about coordinating an adult work camp? or helping to plan a mission saturation event? or attending a school of missions?

Are you interested in evangelism? Would you assist in developing a shepherding program? or help research the unchurched in the area? or lead a study in discipleship?

The point, obviously, is that not everyone has the same interests. And aren't we grateful for that! We need a variety of talents and a variety of interests, as Paul so dramatically and humorously points out in 1 Corinthians 12. Can you imagine the whole body being an eye, he asks? or an ear? We can laugh at the ludicrousness of such a situation and can affirm with him that many members, many talents, and many interests working together make up the Body of Christ.

The key, of course, is to make sure that the involvement is meaningful. Don't ask someone who hates computers to do data entry or someone with stage fright to be worship leader. No one enjoys being asked to do something which makes her or him uncomfortable.

Exciting things begin to happen, however, when people are asked to do things which are meaningful and enjoyable to them. Interest in the church grows, attitudes change, and commitment level increases.

A recently published report underlines this truth. The report summarizes the findings of a study on the current giving behavior of Americans. An important revelation, according to the authors, is the correlation between involvement and giving. Regardless of income, occupation, educational level, or age, those who volunteer their time also give a higher proportion of their income to charity. In fact, "the percentage of income contributed increases directly with the number of hours volunteered."[6] The report further suggests that there is a significant capacity to increase giving if more persons would become involved in the life and work of charitable organizations.[7] The report's findings have important implications for the church. On the one hand the report suggests that people who are involved in at least one other activity besides Sunday morning worship are likely to be better givers. The greater the involvement, the greater the likelihood of increased gifts. On the other hand, if interests are not matched or involvement is not high, the likelihood is that any giving will be token giving.

Church leaders should thus strive to involve members as fully as possible in the life of the church. In so doing, the leaders will be developing loyal and faithful supporters who respond out of their total being.

5. *Investment.* If potential donors have been appropriately identified, informed, and involved in the life of the church in ways that are of interest to them, there is a good probability that they also will be willing to invest their financial resources generously. Persons tend to invest the most charitable dollars where they also invest their time and talent.

Sometimes interest and involvement are so high that people will take the initiative in making substantial gifts without even being asked. Clarence Tompkins tells the marvelous story of how he once asked a university president the reason for his obvious fund raising successes. The president's reply was that he never asked for money. Rather, he would take potential donors on a tour of the campus and share with them his dreams. Time after time persons with resources would help make those dreams a reality.[8] In addition to sharing his dreams, this president was obviously savvy enough to do his homework and make sure his dreams coincided with potential donor interests. His approach also provided persons with opportunities, not desperate needs.

The president's method may well sound like the ideal situation, but fund raising doesn't always happen that way! When it doesn't come so easily, which may be the majority of the time, church leaders must not forget to invite persons to make an investment of their financial resources.

Asking for money is by far the most difficult step for most people. How many times have you heard people say, "I'll do anything you want as long as it isn't asking for money"? Few people are comfortable initially in asking others for gifts, but the skill can be learned. If it is not, the cultivation cycle breaks down at this point, and the potential for major gift support is significantly weakened.

Someone once put the whole process of asking for gifts in proper perspective by raising the question, "What is the worst thing that can happen?" The worst thing that can happen is that someone can say "no," which is hardly the end of the world. If church leaders can learn not to take refusals personally and can learn to see requests as invitations, the whole process can be not only endurable but actually enjoyable. This step is simply sharing an opportunity and inviting a response, not demanding a ransom. The invitation to invest is an invitation to glorify God, serve neighbor, and find personal fulfillment. Could there be a more worthy and satisfying endeavor?

These five steps (identification, information, interest, involvement, and investment) should comprise a continuing cycle as leaders constantly seek to develop and nurture members who are involved and committed to the mission of the church. Because these steps form the basic foundation for any fund raising strategy, they will be referred to again in later chapters.

In addition to these five essential steps in fund raising, three essential components make up a well-rounded fund raising program. These components are annual gifts, capital gifts, and planned gifts.

Annual gifts are those gifts received and used in any given year for the current expenses of an organization. In the church, annual gifts go toward the mission program—local, national, and international—as well as toward staff salaries, heat, lights, and maintenance of facilities. Chapter 5 will focus on developing an effective annual giving program.

Capital gifts are those gifts received and used for special projects over and above the annual budget. In the church, capital gifts might be received for the renovation or expansion of existing facilities or for the building of new facilities. Capital gifts also might be received for endowment purposes. Chapter 6 will focus on developing an effective capital gifts program.

Planned gifts are those gifts which are made during a person's lifetime but received at the time of death, such as gifts through wills, insurance, gift annuities, and trusts. Such gifts can be used for either annual or capital purposes, depending upon the wishes of the donor and the policies of the church. Chapter 7 will focus on developing an effective planned gifts program.

TO SUMMARIZE

An attitude of love is the most important element for Christians engaged in fund raising. This attitude should be informed and inspired by the gospel and should help one see giving as an opportunity, not an imposition. Such an attitude grows out of a recognition of God's unconditional love and is further nurtured through prayer, study, and actual practice in giving.

A dozen other qualities are also needed by church leaders in order to present positively the invitation to grow in stewardship of one's financial resources. These qualities are honesty, compassion, care, integrity, accountability, vision, communication skills, optimism, enthusiasm, sensitivity, listening skills, and patience. Because these qualities are readily present in many church leaders, the basic foundation is there for effective leadership in fund raising.

Fund raising is a continuing cycle involving five major steps: identification of potential donors, gathering information from and sharing information with these persons, learning about their interests, encouraging meaningful involvement in the life of the church, and inviting their investment of resources.

The three essential components of a well-rounded fund raising program are annual gifts, capital gifts, and planned gifts.

Chapter Four

STRATEGIES FOR FUND RAISING

"To convert ideas and good intentions into something real and positive requires time and perseverance."

Eugenio Mendoza[1]

As church leaders seek to develop a vision and plan for the church's future which is big enough and bold enough to capture people's attention and commitment, they would do well to remember Mendoza's words. Such a vision cannot be thrown together quickly, but grows out of extensive discussion, assessment, and planning. No shortcuts can be taken.

Although there are no shortcuts and no substitutes for hard work, perseverance, and time, there are some well-defined stages an organization must move through in developing a compelling plan for the future. The first part of Chapter 4 outlines these stages. The latter part of this chapter presents some guidelines for using this plan once it is prepared.

The strategies outlined in this chapter can be helpful to a church whether it is looking to strengthen its annual gifts, seek capital gifts, or launch a planned gifts program. Indeed, most churches would benefit from undertaking this planning process. Not only would their financial support likely increase, but also their clarity of mission would be significantly enhanced.

Six stages can be identified in developing a compelling and persuasive invitation to support the church's ministries:

1. Getting organized
2. Developing a mission statement
3. Assessing the environment
4. Formulating goals

5. Developing fund raising goals
6. Preparing a case statement

Let us look at each one in depth.

1. *Getting organized.* Although this sounds simple enough, getting organized may actually be the most difficult part of the whole process. To get organized means first of all to get a commitment from key leaders to engage in an extensive planning process. Many churches have a tradition of doing things as they've always been done, and leaders may think it is unnecessary to engage in such planning. If this is the case, discussion needs to take place about the potential benefits and drawbacks. Benefits could include such items as providing an opportunity to clarify the church's mission, stimulate forward thinking, solve organizational problems, develop concrete goals, and build teamwork. Drawbacks could be that planning will consume time and energy, may move the church in new directions where some are not prepared to go, and may call into question some of the church's current programs.

If those involved in leadership are willing seriously to consider such planning as an option, they may wish to educate themselves further about the planning process. Many denominational offices have materials and personnel available to assist local churches in their planning. Books, seminars, and consultants are available as well. If the church has not engaged in such planning before, leaders might find a good book and perhaps an outside facilitator very helpful. Using outside help can free leaders to be active participants rather than simply to be managers of a process.

Assuming that the leadership decides to engage in the planning process, the next question to face in getting organized is, Who will do the planning? Rather than giving the responsibility of planning to an existing committee, the church would be well served if a special committee were formed specifically for this purpose. It might well become a permanent committee within the structure of the church and could be known as the strategic planning committee, the long-range planning committee, or simply the planning committee. In this book it will be referred to hereafter as the planning committee. The purpose of this committee is to determine where the church should be in the future and how it will get there.

Obviously the key leadership of the church should be involved in the

40

planning committee. The pastor and key board representatives should be included, as well as others who could bring different viewpoints and yet function well as a team. A good size for a planning committee is five to eight members, though it might be as small as three persons or as large as twelve, depending upon the size of the church. The committee would, of course, solicit input from a wide variety of committees and organizations within the church as it prepared its plan.

Another question to be addressed is, How far in the future do we plan? Normally, planning committees find it reasonable to project three to five years into the future. This committee would be responsible for developing goals for the church for that time period, which would become the church's long-range plan. The committee would also develop short-term goals of one to two years duration which would lead the church toward the fulfillment of its long-term goals.

Finally, the question should be addressed regarding how long the planning process will take. No simple answer can be given to this question, as time spent in the planning process varies enormously from organization to organization. Some consultants suggest that a minimum of eight hours (spread over several meetings) is needed to do an adequate job of planning and that this time could extend to more than forty hours of meetings for those choosing to do extensive planning. Most church planning committees probably will find they can do their task in eight to twelve hours if they rely on other committees within the church for data and information.

Once the initial planning is done, the long-range goals should be reviewed at least annually by the planning committee, and new short-term goals should be established at that time. The entire process of creating new long-range goals should be done in three- to five-year intervals or when the previous goals are completed. Thus, the planning process is never completed, but is an ongoing tool to assist the church in fulfilling its mission.

2. *Developing a mission statement.* Defining the church's mission is the first major task of the planning committee. The mission statement becomes the foundation for the entire planning process and therefore needs the careful attention of the planning committee.

Dennis J. Murray succinctly defines what a mission statement is: "The mission statement describes why the organization exists, its philosophy and heritage, the current scope of its operations, its primary programs and services, the clients it aims to serve, its style of management, and its aspirations."[2] He further suggests that such a statement should be clear and concise enough to guide all major decision making within an organization.

Murray's definition provides the framework for the planning committee to evaluate and update an existing mission statement or to develop one if none exists. By answering the following questions, the committee would be well on the way toward developing a workable mission statement.

Why does the organization exist? Every organization was formed for a reason. When and why was this church formed, and what was its original mission? Is that mission still valid today? If not, how has it changed? A review of its history can help a church reaffirm its original mission or, if that mission is no longer valid, intentionally adopt a revised mission. Oftentimes in asking questions about its own history, a church rediscovers some marvelous stories of its beginnings, stories of dedication and commitment which can help shape future aspirations.

What is the organization's philosophy and heritage? Is this church part of a larger denominational body? If so, who were the founders of the denomination? What were their major beliefs? What are the distinguishing marks philosophically and theologically of the denomination today? The mission statement should recognize the denominational tradition of the church and how this influences the local church's understanding of its mission.

Likewise, the mission statement should lift up any distinguishing characteristics of the local church's heritage. Are there significant traditions, values, or ministries that have persisted over time that distinguish it from other churches in the area? What makes this local church unique?

What is the current scope of the organization? What important ministries does the church provide for its own members? What ministries does it provide for the community? To what extent is it engaged in national and international ministries? Answering these questions helps the church understand the breadth and depth of its mission.

What are the primary programs or services of the organization? What is it that members point to with pride when they tell others about this church? Is the church known for any outstanding or unique

42

programs? Which programs and services are considered most important by various leaders within the church? In answering these questions, the purpose is not to develop a long list of programs, but to identify how specific programs and services are helping the church accomplish its mission and meet identified needs.

Who are the primary clients served by the organization? Does the church draw its membership from a defined geographical area? Is its membership notably from one age bracket or racial group? Are its programs and services primarily for certain groups of people, whether or not from its own membership? No church can be all things to all people. Answering these questions helps a church identify its particular niche and focus its programs and services on those who are its primary clients.

What is the organization's style of management? Is the church autonomous or part of a larger connectional system? How does this affect its decision making and its management style? Who is the decision-making body on the local level? Finding the answers to these questions enables the planning committee to understand how change takes place within the church.

What are the organization's aspirations? The mission statement is primarily a forward-looking document. Its emphasis is not on where the organization has been, but on where it is going. Thus, the planning committee needs to ask: What are our dreams for the future? What do we believe God wants this church to be five years from now? Whom will we be serving? Addressing these questions will ensure that the church leaders look to the future and seek to discern God's will as they prepare for new challenges and opportunities.

As the above questions indicate, the task of preparing the mission statement is serious business, requiring time, thought, and effort. The process may well be as important as the product and should not be rushed. As the planning committee researches the church's origins, gathers data, and interviews people in order to answer the questions, it will undoubtedly gain a clearer sense of both the church's history and its potential for future service.

Understanding the church so well could be either disturbing or heartening. Some churches, for example, have lost all sense of mission other than their own survival. To confront this reality is to recognize that unless they reaffirm their original mission or redefine their mission to be much deeper and broader than their own institutional survival, they have no legitimate reason to exist. Other churches will discover that the process of preparing a mission statement affirms a variety of ways they are in mission and challenges them to build upon this.

The actual writing of the mission statement should be assigned to one person after the planning committee has thoroughly discussed the questions and sought input from others. The goal should be to develop a concise statement of one or two paragraphs, or one page at most, highlighting the church's reason for existence and how it intends to carry out its mission in the present and the future.

A draft document should be brought back to the planning committee for review and revision. When the committee is satisfied that the document represents the committee's understanding of the mission and purpose of the church, the writing should be circulated widely within the church for comment and clarification. Changes, if merited, can again be made, and then the document should be sent to the governing board for their approval. Once approved, the mission statement should be made available to all members and should be used regularly as the standard by which new programs and services are judged as either appropriate or inappropriate to the church's basic mission.

3. *Assessing the environment.* Once the mission statement is in place, the planning committee should seek to assess the environment—both today's environment and tomorrow's probable environment—to discover the major challenges and opportunities facing the church. The committee should look at factors both outside the church (external assessment) and inside the church (internal assessment).

In conducting the assessment the committee again should rely on interviews with other individuals and groups within the church as well as on the knowledge of those on the committee. Individuals on the committee should also familiarize themselves with literature that could assist them in understanding future trends and directions.

Beginning with external assessment, the committee should seek to identify the major threats and opportunities in the environment which could influence the church's ministry in the years ahead. Philip Kotler suggests that each threat should be assessed according to two dimensions: its potential severity and its probability of occurrence. Likewise, each opportunity should be assessed according to its potential attractiveness and its probability of success.[3] The committee should aim to list four or five major threats and/or opportunities which could be considered in long-range planning. In doing its external assessment, the committee may find it helpful to focus on the following areas:

Needs of people. What are the unmet needs of people in the congregation and in the area the church serves? How are these needs changing? What new needs will emerge in the next five years? A church may list as a threat the fact that many older people in the congregation are moving away, leading to a declining interest in its programs for the elderly. That same congregation may list as an opportunity the fact that young families are moving into the area, bringing with them needs for a church home, an active education program, and daycare for their children.

Competitors. Are there other organizations providing the same programs or services? If so, this could be a threat or an opportunity. If another organization is providing the same service, then maybe the church should no longer be involved. Or the opportunity may exist to team up with the other organization to provide the service in a better manner than either could do alone. For example, a church may need to decide whether to continue its food pantry ministry as is, quit it all together, or join forces with several other churches in the area with similar programs.

Environmental forces. Kotler suggests the main environmental forces that have to be watched are the demographic, economic, technological, political, and social. "These forces largely represent 'uncontrollables' in the organization's situation to which it has to adapt."[4] For example, a threat to a church might be the proposed closing of a major industry which employs a number of the church's members. A church might regard the technological advances in satellite television as an opportunity, providing the occasion for enhanced educational and religious programming.

Following the external assessment, the planning committee should conduct an internal assessment in which it seeks to identify the church's strengths and weaknesses, again listing the top four or five the committee might want to consider in long-range planning. The committee may find this assessment helpful in preparing such a list to focus on the following areas:

Programs. How does each program contribute to the mission of the church? Are there programs which have fulfilled their purpose and should be phased out? Are there other programs or services not being

45

performed which should be considered? Earlier, the example was given of a church recognizing the need for daycare services among the young families moving into the area. In conducting its internal assessment, that church may want to consider whether its resources would be suited for developing such a program.

Personnel. Is the size of the staff adequate for the projected future? Does the staff have the appropriate skills, enthusiasm, and dedication for the tasks to be done? If new programs are added, how will this influence staffing needs? A church may list as a strength the loyalty, skills, and stability of its staff. It may list as a weakness that no one on the professional staff has the necessary time or training to strengthen the educational program.

Physical Plant. Are the facilities adequate for the foreseeable future? Is there flexibility to accommodate new programs or services? Are any major construction or renovation needs anticipated? A church might list as a strength that the education wing is under-utilized and could accommodate a daycare center. It might note as a weakness that the pipe organ is in bad disrepair, requiring major rebuilding or replacement.

Finances. Are the finances adequate for the current programs of the church? Is there any flexibility to take on new projects? Does the church anticipate any major changes in funding patterns over the next several years? Here our hypothetical church might note as a strength that a daycare center would generate additional revenues which could be used for new programming. The church might list as a weakness that either rebuilding or replacing the pipe organ would be a major expenditure.

The final step in the assessment process is to review the list of threats and opportunities, strengths and weaknesses, and to identify six to eight of the most critical factors that should be considered in the long-range plan. This summary then should be shared with the governing board for its review and input in preparation for the next stage.

4. *Formulating goals.* The assessment process provides the church with the necessary background to formulate goals. The purpose in developing goals is to keep the church from drifting into an uncertain future. By developing concrete goals which build upon internal strengths and external opportunities, the church will be in a position to

help shape the future rather than simply be shaped by it. Goals assist the church in developing effective plans to accomplish its mission.

The task of the planning committee is to formulate some broad long-range goals for the next three to five years. Each goal then is passed on to an appropriate committee within the church for further study. Its task is to identify various strategies for accomplishing the goal and to recommend the best strategy. Once its recommendation has received the approval of the board, the committee recommending the strategy would be charged with developing detailed plans to accomplish the recommended strategy.

Ultimately the mission statement, the broad goals, and the detailed plans should be brought together in one document to form the long-range plan. This document should be reviewed annually to evaluate progress toward the goals and to revise strategies as necessary.

The planning committee should develop its long-range goals from the list of six to eight critical factors that emerge from the assessment. In developing goals, the committee will want to focus on its mission statement, opportunities which complement the church's strengths, and threats which cannot be ignored. The committee should limit the number of long-range goals, recognizing that it is better to accomplish a few well-chosen goals than to create many goals which dissipate the church's strengths and have little likelihood of being accomplished.

In formulating goals, the planning committee should remember the following guidelines. Goals should be

> *Written*—Writing forces the goal to be clear and concise.
> *Specific*—Goals should answer the questions, who? what? and when?
> *Positive*—Goals should be stated positively rather than negatively.
> *Compatible*—Goals should be compatible with one another.
> *Attainable*—Goals should be stretching but realistic.
> *Verifiable*—One should be able to evaluate if goals have been met.

Our hypothetical church might list as its long-range goals the following:

> *a.* To have a fine working pipe organ by (three years from now). Committee responsible: worship committee.

47

 b. To strengthen the Christian education program by (two years from now). Committee responsible: education committee.

 c. To assist in meeting the community's need for daycare services by (three years from now). Committee responsible: evangelism committee.

 d. To strengthen the church's program for the hungry by (two years from now). Committee responsible: missions committee.

 e. To assist in preparing future leaders for the church by (three years from now). Committee responsible: finance committee.

5. *Developing fund raising goals.* Let's assume that the various committees did their homework and developed appropriate strategies to meet the long-range goals. These committees also would be asked to build dollar estimates for each strategy. The purpose would be to determine the financial resources needed to accomplish each long-range goal.

For example, the worship committee of our hypothetical church may determine, after appropriate consultation, that rebuilding the existing organ is feasible. The committee receives estimates from various organ builders and determines that the cost would be approximately $150,000. The education committee proposes hiring a part-time director of Christian education and purchasing a satellite television dish to make available national religious education programming. This committee also determines that approximately $7,000 would be needed for a director of Christian education and $3,000 would be needed for a television satellite dish. In a similar manner, the other committees would seek to build dollar estimates for each of their strategies.

The planning committee would then develop fund raising goals from these estimates. Their goals might look something like the following:

 a. To raise $150,000 for rebuilding the pipe organ.

 b. To raise $10,000 for strengthening the Christian education program.

 c. To raise $10,000 for establishing a daycare center at the church.

 d. To raise $10,000 for developing an interdenominational ministry to the hungry.

e. To raise $50,000 for establishing a scholarship program at a nearby seminary.

The planning committee would suggest to the board an overall goal of $230,000 to be raised within three years in order to accomplish the long-range goals of the church.

Raising money is thus not an end in itself, but a means of meeting important goals. Such a statement seems self-evident, but it is critically important. Fund raising goals must always grow out of organizational goals. To seek funds with little idea about how they will be used is self-defeating, for donors do not simply give money away. However, they do respond to challenging ideas and programs that are consistent with their own interests and values. The church that carefully develops such programs in a manner similar to that described above and then attaches legitimate fund raising goals to these programs is in a good position to receive support. Before inviting such support, however, the planning committee has one more task.

6. *Preparing a case statement.* The case statement is the culmination of all the planning, assessment, and goal setting that has gone on before. This document is used internally and externally and becomes a primary tool for raising awareness and funds. A case statement may take many forms during the fund raising process, but in all forms it should be a clear, succinct, and compelling statement of who the church is, what it seeks to do, and why it deserves support.

How is a case statement prepared? Like the mission statement, the case statement should be written initially by one person. That person should have the ability to tell the church's story in a motivating manner. The case statement should be brief and should contain the following items:

a. A description of the church and its ministries. It is important to provide perspective and to indicate how the church has met, and continues to meet, clearly defined needs. Significant past accomplishments might be noted here.
b. A description of continuing and new needs to be addressed by the church. Here the goals identified in long-range planning are spelled out, indicating how they will meet identified needs and assist the church in fulfilling its mission.
c. A description of the fund raising goals. The amount of money

49

needed for each component is listed, as well as the total goal, and the importance and urgency of raising this money in order for the church to fulfill its mission are emphasized.

d. A plan of action for accomplishing these goals. A brief overview of the timeline and organizational structure for raising the money is given. The purposes are to underscore the urgency of this effort and to demonstrate that the endeavor is carefully planned.

e. A listing of key people who endorse the goals. Those who are providing leadership in this effort should be identified. Testimonials from key individuals who support the goals or from those who benefit from the church's ministries can be powerful motivators in the case statement.

f. An outline of how one can give. The range of gifts needed as well as the various methods for making gifts can be listed. Opportunities for making commemorative or memorial gifts also should be noted. The purpose is to stress that every gift is important and can make a difference.

The case statement thus becomes the church's story, pointing to a vision of what the church can be, and inviting support for making it happen. If the above stages are followed faithfully and the case statement is prepared carefully, this story should be big enough and bold enough to claim the attention and commitment of many individuals.

Let's look then at some of the ways the case statement can be helpful in telling the church's story and in inviting response. The case statement can be used in at least five ways:[5]

1. *To involve key leaders and build consensus.* After the first draft is written, it should be shared among key leaders within the church for their review and comments. Allowing several people to review the draft enables the church's story to be strengthened as new ideas and suggestions are incorporated into revised versions. Reading and critiquing various drafts also helps to build consensus among the leaders regarding the organizational and financial goals.

2. *To recruit volunteer leadership.* Again in the early stages of its development, the case statement can be used as a tool to recruit volunteers for the fund raising effort. The case statement is shared with potential volunteers in draft form, and their reactions and their assistance are invited in refining the document. As they have an

opportunity to ask questions and participate in perfecting the final document, many will develop ownership in the goals and can be recruited as enthusiastic volunteers to assist in the fund raising.

3. *To test the market.* The key leaders in the church develop consensus around the organizational and financial goals as they participate in the various stages of planning and as they review various drafts of the case statement. However, a fund raising effort will not be successful unless there is broad consensus that the goals are compelling and timely. Hence, testing the market is essential. The case statement, again in draft form, should be shared with a number of potential major donors who have not been involved in the planning process. They should be invited to share their reactions, to indicate which areas are of particular interest to them, and to suggest additional goals which might strengthen the case or have even greater appeal to them or others. The hope for testing the market is that it will reveal a broad base of support for the goals. If such support is not gained, however, the church leaders may need to rethink their plans.

4. *To obtain major leadership gifts.* Once the case statement has been widely shared in draft form, there should be an awareness of who the major supporters are. Those who can help set the pace of the fund raising effort by making major leadership commitments should be invited to do so. Again the case statement can play an important role. Inviting persons to make leadership gifts should always be done face-to-face and should be personalized as much as possible. The case statement can also be personalized with a cover sheet and an attached proposal keyed to the donor's particular interests. This personalized approach will help major donors see that their support is critical to the success of the effort.

5. *To invite support from a broad base of people.* Finally, the case statement should be mass-produced in an attractive manner so that it can be used to inform the entire constituency of the church's goals and to invite its support.

Probably not everyone can be visited. However, support for the goals will be enhanced if opportunities are created which allow people to ask questions and be heard. Oftentimes an attractive climate is created when groups of people are brought together and the case statement is used as a support piece to accompany personal testimonies from those who have made leadership commitments. Such an atmosphere of dialogue and testimony often generates a spirit of enthusiasm that inspires those present to "get on board." For those who live at a distance or are unable to attend a group gathering, the case statement can be mailed along with a cover letter inviting their support.

In addition to the printed case statement, some organizations have found it helpful to make a videotape which presents the case. A videotape can be used in personal visits and group settings or can even be sent in the mail instead of the printed document.

The case statement allows the church to tell its story again and again in many different settings and in a variety of ways. Nothing is magical about a case statement. However, for those who have wrestled with their mission, identified critical needs that they can address, and developed thoughtful plans and strategies for doing so, the case statement becomes a useful tool for presenting a vision and inviting a response.

This planning process is appropriate for a church of any size. Likewise, the case statement is a valid fund raising tool for both small and large financial goals. It makes no difference whether a church has a membership of 30, 300, or 3,000, or a financial goal of $23,000, $230,000 or $2,300,000. The planning that results in a case statement is a necessary process for developing a vision that will capture the attention and commitment of church members.

TO SUMMARIZE

Developing a vision for the church which can attract people's attention and commitment is no easy task; it takes time and effort. Leaders of churches willing to invest themselves in this task, however, will be amply rewarded with a clearer sense of their church's mission and specific goals to move the church toward deeper fulfillment of that mission.

A church must go through several stages to reach this point. First, the leadership of the church must commit itself to a time of extensive planning and must get organized for such planning. Second, a mission statement for the church needs to be developed; third, an assessment needs to be done; fourth, long-range goals need to be formulated; and fifth, fund raising goals need to emerge from the long-range goals.

Finally, a case statement needs to be prepared. This statement becomes the means for presenting the church's vision and inviting a response. The statement will be the church's basic fund raising tool, but it will be effective only to the degree that it grows out of the previous stages.

Chapter Five

DEVELOPING AN EFFECTIVE ANNUAL GIVING PROGRAM

"Fund promotion at its best is faithful to the highest criteria of what constitutes good education."

Joe W. Walker[1]

In Chapter 1, Bob Allen, senior pastor at Christ Church, described his church's $100,000 shortfall in the annual budget. He is not alone with this problem, of course. Many churches face deficits each year in their annual budgets and end up resorting to special offerings and year-end appeals to "balance the budget." A sigh of relief is heard when enough is received to pay the bills for another year. Often the cycle repeats itself a year later.

A strong annual giving program is the foundation for a well-balanced stewardship program and should be in place before a church seeks to embark on a capital gifts program or a planned gifts program. But how is a strong annual giving program built? There must be a better way than last-minute pleas to meet the budget.

The better way to meet the budget is offered by Manfred Holck, Jr. He writes, "The solution to the desperate needs of many congregations is in an effective year-round stewardship program that challenges the membership to think creatively about the way in which they give and the amount that they give."[2] Rather than simply relying on an annual fund drive, weekly offerings, and then crisis appeals, the church which is serious about developing strong stewardship will be equally serious about developing a strong stewardship education program.

The primary purpose of stewardship education is not to finance the church budget, but to help Christians grow in their understanding of God's love, to help them look seriously at their stewardship of time and life and money, and to help them grow in grace as they learn to respond more freely and fully to God's love for them. When Christians learn to give wholeheartedly in response to God's love, the budget needs of the church will be readily met.

Thus, the focus of stewardship education is not on the need of the church to receive, but on the need of Christians to give. Through stewardship education we learn that the only appropriate response to God who gave all is to give of ourselves—our time, our money, and our talents—as generously as we can to further God's work. Our gifts then become a natural response to God's redemptive gift. They also become symbols of our commitment and priorities. And the church becomes a channel to receive and administer these gifts for God's work.

The need for such education is clear. In a recent survey, 41 percent of those who contributed financially to churches could not articulate any biblical guidelines or principles for doing so.[3] From this statistic we can see that one cannot assume that Christian principles are the key motivating factors for many who give to the church. Seen in this light, church deficits should come as no surprise. The real surprise is that churches manage as well as they do, given the large number of people who make token gifts rather than gifts growing out of a recognition that all of life belongs to God.

An effective stewardship education program will seek to inform, to inspire, and to challenge. Persons need first to be informed about the biblical and theological reasons for giving. They also need to be informed about the opportunities for giving that the church provides and about what their gifts are accomplishing.

Information, however, is not enough. Persons also need to be inspired. They need to be inspired by the biblical message of stewardship. They need to be inspired by the testimonies of those who have discovered the joy of giving generously. And they need to be inspired by stories of persons who have been helped and of lives that have been changed by their gifts.

Ultimately, persons in the church need to be challenged. They need to be challenged to see that the size of their gifts is not dependent upon the size of the church budget, but upon how much God has entrusted to them. They need to be challenged to see the tithe not as a threat but as a benchmark to aim toward, and even surpass, as they seek to give all they can to Christ who gave his all. And they need to be challenged to make a commitment which is worthy of their Christian calling.

Fran Alguire tells of an incident which demonstrates how persons of all ages can make commitments worthy of their Christian calling when they are appropriately informed, inspired, and challenged. Her grand-daughter, Anna, age eight, often gives more than a tithe from her nickel-and-dime allowance. Recently she presented Fran with 38 cents in small coins "for missions." Fran asked her, "Do you want this to go for homeless people, hospitals in Africa, or buying fish to stock ponds to feed the hungry?" Anna replied, "Just a minute," and returned shortly with 29 cents more, making a total of 67 cents to be divided three ways. She found each item so important that her initial gift was instantly almost doubled so she could support all three. What an exciting example of stewardship education in action!

What would a year-round stewardship education program look like? Many years ago Charlie Shedd outlined a program he developed for his local church.[4] The model was simple, straightforward, and effective. It merits our attention yet today. Shedd recommended the following:

Each week a statement should be included in the church bulletin on the subject of stewardship and the importance of percentage giving.

Each month percentage giving should be mentioned from the pulpit during the announcement period in an attractive and interesting way. This announcement might take the form of a scriptural reference or a human interest story.

Each quarter a five- to ten-minute personal testimony on giving should be made by laypersons to Sunday school classes.

Twice a year the pastor should deliver a stewardship sermon with an emphasis on percentage giving. Also, two times a year a letter should go out to the entire congregation from church officials commending percentage giving as a way to grow in grace.

Once a year every organization in the church should have a brief presentation on tithing from a key leader in the church.

Shedd recognizes that casual giving habits do not change overnight and that constant repetition of the stewardship message in an attractive manner is essential for people to begin to change their ways. His patience and persistence toward that end are evident in his original name for this program: A Twenty-Year Program of Stewardship Training.

Shedd also recognized that a continuous program of stewardship education cannot be carried out by one person alone, but requires ownership and involvement by the church's key leadership. Thus, he sought the endorsement of the church's governing board for this

57

program. A brochure outlining the program was prepared and distributed to church members; a committee on tithing was created to oversee the program; and a motto was adopted which summarized the program's philosophy: "We are not concerned with your share of our budget—what really matters is God's share of your income."

Finally, Shedd recognized that in order to be effective, a stewardship education program needs to start where the people are. Rather than insisting that all members must tithe, the approach adopted by his church was "Study the scriptures and see what Christ says to you; start somewhere and develop as the Lord leads."

Was the program effective? During an eight-year period, membership increased more than 26 percent; the operating budget increased more than 400 percent; and benevolent giving increased from 15 to 50 percent of the budget. Equally important, Shedd witnessed amazing results in the spiritual development of individuals and renewed interest in the work of the church, which led to increased dedication of time and talents. Although such dramatic results cannot be promised to every church which embarks on such a program, the approach Shedd outlines is solid and can provide a good foundation for a continuing program of stewardship education.

In addition to Shedd's suggestions, those embarking on a continuous stewardship education program might also want to consider the following:

More effective use of the offertory. In many churches, the offertory is placed haphazardly in the worship service, with little thought given to its educational and theological functions. In a majority of churches the offering is received with little or no comment, thus reducing what could and should be a central part of the worship service to a mundane appendage.

To make more effective use of the offertory means first to recognize the tremendous educational possibilities inherent in this part of worship. A marvelous opportunity exists each week to interpret biblical passages on giving, to develop a theology of giving, and to share the good news about what the church's gifts are accomplishing. The offertory also can be a time to lift up new opportunities for mission, to hear personal stories from those who have grown in their stewardship, and to thank the faithful for the commitment demonstrated through their weekly offerings.

Likewise, the opportunity exists following the receiving of the offering to express gratitude to God for all of life, and to dedicate the gifts to the purpose of furthering God's work. Prayers of gratitude and dedication move the offertory from an incidental part of the service to the high point of the service, where members can respond to the gospel by dedicating their gifts *and themselves* to God's work.

Eugene Brand describes this potential power of the offertory when he writes: "The offering is thus a symbolic action. The gifts are offered in token of our self-offering. With them we mean to lay ourselves upon God's altar, to be at God's service. The offering, then, responds to God with a pledge of servanthood. It is a symbolic gesture of surrender and thus of the obedient will."[5]

Recognizing the offertory as a gesture of surrender has implications for its placement in the worship service. To suggest that the offertory should occur only one place in the service would be inappropriate, but its placement should be considered carefully, not for the sake of convenience, but for the opportunity it provides persons to respond, concretely and symbolically, to God's Word. It would seem to be especially appropriate following the hearing of God's Word either in the scriptures or in the sermon.

The offertory thus provides a fitting way to respond to the good news and to rededicate one's life and one's resources to God. The offering need not be limited solely to receiving money. Periodically the church may want to find ways to invite persons symbolically to rededicate time and talents to God as well. With some thought and planning, the offertory can become a powerful opportunity both to teach stewardship and to demonstrate stewardship in action.

Periodic study groups. Although the worship service can be an appropriate place to raise awareness of stewardship principles and responsibilities, it does not provide the opportunity for indepth study and discussion. Thus, a church may want to consider offering short-term study opportunities on a regular basis which focus on some aspect of stewardship. An initial study might be offered on the meaning of stewardship. This could be followed by further studies which would focus on specific areas such as the stewardship of time, the stewardship of talents, the stewardship of natural resources, and the stewardship of money.

Not everyone in the church would choose to participate in these studies, of course. Nonetheless, such studies could have a leavening influence on the church as more persons come to an understanding of and appreciation for the biblical concept of stewardship.

Covenant/prayer groups. The ultimate goal of stewardship education is not simply understanding or appreciating stewardship, but committing oneself to a lifestyle of stewardship. Such commitment can be greatly strengthened if it is supported by others making similar commitments. Thus, the church may want to provide leadership in establishing covenant/prayer groups for persons who are prepared to take the next step toward a stewardship lifestyle.

At the conclusion of short-term studies, the concept of covenant/ prayer groups could be explained by the group leader as an opportunity to put learning into practice and to support one another in the process. Interested persons would be invited to covenant together to practice certain stewardship disciplines, such as giving a certain percentage of their income to the church, doing volunteer work a certain number of hours each week, and using one or more of their talents each week to serve others. They also would agree to meet regularly over a period of time to experience mutual support and accountability, to pray together, to read the scriptures, and to share the joys and concerns of their stewardship journeys.

Again, the leavening influence of such groups on the church would far outweigh the numbers involved; thus the church should encourage, support, and provide leadership for them even if only a few individuals are interested initially.

Some undoubtedly will resist a continuous stewardship education program, suggesting it is excessive and places undue emphasis on money. These persons should be reminded of Jesus' own emphasis on this subject. They should be helped to see that stewardship is a way of life and that a giving lifestyle is at the center of the Christian faith. Growing in stewardship is nothing less than growing in discipleship, and growing in discipleship means growing in stewardship. Isn't the church called to nurture such growth?

Indeed, churches which fail to provide continuous stewardship education are doing their members a disservice. In these churches members are not regularly exposed to Christian concepts of how to use their resources (though they are bombarded daily with secular understandings of what to do with their resources); they are not regularly challenged to grow to new levels of Christian commitment; they are deprived of the spiritual blessings which accompany increased commitment; and the church is weakened in the ministries it provides. The real question to be asked is, can the church devote itself to anything less than continuous stewardship education and still be faithful to its mission?

Those churches that do provide an effective year-round program of stewardship education will have a strong foundation for their annual giving program. Although they still should plan to have an annual commitment drive, it will not be crisis-oriented nor will it emphasize the church budget. Rather an annual commitment drive will grow out of long-range planning and year-round stewardship education. The planning and education emphases will provide ample opportunity to interpret the stewardship message, communicate what the church is doing, and challenge people in their giving. The annual commitment drive becomes the opportunity to invite a response. Herbert Mather aptly describes this as "the 'altar call' at the end of a time of interpretation, communication, and challenge."[6]

The purpose of the annual commitment program is to give "each member of the congregation the opportunity to make a personal response—commitment if you please—to the work of the church during the coming year. It is a response to what God has done for us, a response to love, a stewardship response to share what God has entrusted to us."[7] This commitment is known by various names— every member visitation, every member response, annual commitment drive—but whatever the name, the purpose should be the same: to encourage every member to respond to God's love in a concrete way by making a commitment.

Such commitments are important to the church as it seeks to plan and manage its ministry programs in a responsible manner. People who resist making commitments to the church might be reminded that they make pledges and commitments to other institutions all the time; they commit to mortgage companies, to banks, to jobs, to spouses, and to children. Is it any less important to make a commitment to the church?

As important as a commitment is to the church for its planning, it is equally important to the individual making the commitment. Our faith demands commitment. In making a financial commitment to the church, we are forced to turn our lives outward, to demonstrate what we really believe, and to give external evidence of our internal priorities. Our faith calls us to be Christians in deed, and not word only. Making a commitment helps us to put our faith into practice.

Five essential steps lead to a successful annual commitment drive. These steps are preparation, education, invitation, celebration, and evaluation. Let us look at each of these.

1. *Preparation.* Much of the long-range preparation already will have been done by the planning committee (see Chapter 4). In preparing for the annual commitment drive, the long-range plan should be reviewed, and appropriate short-term organizational and fund raising goals should be developed for the next year.

A number of annual commitment programs for churches have been developed by various organizations and are on the market. As a part of the preparation process, the church may wish to review these programs to determine if any seem well suited for its situation. Before choosing any program it should be evaluated by both theological and fund raising criteria. The church needs to ask, for example, if the program emphasizes the joy of giving in response to God's love, or if it promotes giving based on guilt or duty. Likewise, the church should note whether the program seeks to involve donors in any significant way or if it simply seeks a pledge. (For a fuller review of theological criteria, refer to Chapter 2. For a fuller review of fund raising criteria, refer to Chapter 3.)

Such programs do not guarantee success by themselves, but many have been tested in congregational settings and have been found helpful. They can be particularly helpful in providing guidelines for an organizational plan and timeline. Some even provide the publicity. Any program can and should be adapted to the local situation. No program should be seen as a replacement for the key steps of a successful annual commitment drive, but rather as a way to enhance these steps.

An organizational plan and timeline should be prepared following the recommendations of the commitment program, if one is purchased, or building one which is realistic for the church. Three guidelines are worth noting: Allow as much preparation time as possible; keep the organizational structure as simple as possible; and seek to involve as many people as possible in the work of the commitment drive.

A key preparation item is recruiting someone to head the annual commitment drive. This person should be someone who is recognized as a faithful and generous giver and who can effectively recruit others to assist. The recruitment and training of other volunteers is also important. Volunteers are needed to help with each phase of the effort, from preparing publicity to visiting persons and inviting their response. As noted above, the more people involved, the better. Engaging many participants ensures a ready group of workers, involves people in a meaningful way in the work of the church, and is itself an educational experience in stewardship.

A final preparation item is to translate the short-term organizational and fund raising goals into a case statement which can be used to educate the congregation. What are the continuing and new programs that will be accomplished in the year ahead if members respond in loving commitment? The case statement might take the form of a simple brochure that could be used in different settings. Whatever form it takes, the statement should be inspirational as well as informative so that people will want to invest themselves in these programs. (Refer to Chapter 4 for a fuller discussion of the preparation of the case statement.)

Much of a church's annual budget appears fairly mundane at first glance, with such expenses as salaries, utilities, insurance, postage, and office supplies. To simply lift up these items and ask people to support them will hardly generate a lot of enthusiasm. However, these too can be—and should be—translated into programs and services. The church for example, is not simply paying salaries, but is providing leadership for worship and study, for counseling and crisis ministries, and for evangelism and visitation ministries. The church is not simply buying office supplies, but is providing weekly worship bulletins, newsletters, and cassettes of Sunday services for shut-ins.

Harold Seymour, a noted fund raiser, suggests the basic weakness of church annual commitment drives "is that not enough pains are taken to keep program out in front of fund-raising."[8] Some effort is required to translate the budget into opportunities for ministry. However, program and service opportunities rather than line item budgets must be emphasized if people are to catch a vision of what the church can be and to become inspired to help make that vision a reality.

2. *Education.* Educating the congregation about the goals and dreams of the church for the year ahead comes next. The church's creativity can really come out in this area. In addition to the basic brochure, the case statement, churches can prepare audiovisual presen-

63

tations, skits, program booths, mission fairs, testimonial dinners, or whatever method suits them to creatively communicate the story of what they hope to accomplish. The goal is to create a positive and inspiring atmosphere where persons can catch the excitement of a church alive.

As noted in Chapter 4, group settings are particularly conducive to creating such an atmosphere. Some churches have found that congregational dinners followed by a program work especially well. Others have found smaller group meetings in homes to be equally effective. Therefore church leaders should determine what model of small group meetings has the greatest potential for positively involving the largest number of people, and the leaders should develop that model with creativity and enthusiasm.

In addition to group gatherings, church leaders will want to educate the congregation through posters, letters, and other mailings, but these will be secondary to those events which bring people together for dialogue, fellowship, and inspiration.

3. *Invitation.* After members have been told about the church's goals, it is time to invite their response. "There are three ways to ask for support—face-to-face (personal), by telephone, or by mail. Elaborate phonathon efforts and sophisticated direct-mail pieces have achieved important successes. But the history of fund-raising teaches one lesson over and over. Personal solicitation is the strategy for success." [9]

Church leaders have known this; "every member visitation" suggests exactly that. In recent years, however, many churches have moved away from such visitation programs in an effort to find a more efficient way to conduct the annual commitment drive. There may be more efficient ways to manage a drive but none are more effective. A program based on mailed materials alone, for example, offers no opportunity for dialogue or involvement, and positive responses are often insignificant. Again, "experience shows that soliciting a gift personally has a success factor several times greater than a telephone request. Equally important, the gifts are larger." [10]

Traditional fund raising logic suggests that personal visits should be made to key donors and then, if time and volunteers permit, to lesser donors and nondonors. In the church setting, however, it may be equally important to visit those who are not key donors. As Harold

Seymour notes, "the only sure way to move the more remote members of the congregation to higher levels of support is to go out where they are" and see them.[11]

The purpose in seeing them should not be just to receive a financial commitment. It should be a visit where the ministries of the church are enthusiastically shared and individuals are invited to become more deeply involved. It should be a visit where an individual's questions, concerns, joys, and hurts can be shared. Thomas Rieke describes the potential of these visits when he writes: "Let this be a time for beginning again the Christian art of sharing and caring, formed into the human ritual of a visit. It could be precious and priceless. It could change the course of someone's life. And it might change the major direction of your church!"[12]

Thus, a church goal should be to visit as many people as possible during the commitment drive. Visiting is an effective way to tell the church's story which some might not hear in a group setting; it meaningfully involves a number of volunteers and thus deepens the commitment of each; it encourages dialogue and involvement of others; and it opens the door for genuine Christian sharing to take place. On top of all this, a visit is also the most successful method for gaining financial support.

For many people, visiting others is the most threatening part of the commitment drive. It can also be the most rewarding. Several things can be done to help ensure that visiting is a positive, rewarding experience for all.

First, recruit a large number of volunteers to make visits. Those recruited should be the most committed, faithful members of the church. The more who are recruited to call, the better. Ideally, enough people should be recruited so that volunteers would work in teams of two, and each team would need to make only two calls. Conducting visits this way allows plenty of time, so each visit can be a quality visit.

Second, provide plenty of training for the visitors. Training should include a review of all the materials, time for questions and answers, and instructions for making the actual visits. Some churches have found it helpful to demonstrate, through video or role play, the right and wrong ways to make visits. Then those who will make visits are invited to practice making mock visits on one another. Mock visits can be fun and can go a long way toward alleviating any fears people may have.

Third, invite the visitors to make their own commitment first. Part of the visitor training should be the rehearsing once again of the church's story, so that visitors are well prepared to share it with others. Knowing the church's story should also inspire them in their own giving. Some churches have developed a time of worship at the conclusion of the training where the visitors present their own pledge commitments. Worshiping together puts the training in a proper context and also assures a strong start to the commitment drive before any actual calls are made.

Fourth, bring the visitors together again after the visits are made. This meeting ensures that commitments are received as soon as possible by the church and, equally important, provides a time of afterglow for the visitors. As visitors share with one another their positive experiences, the groundwork is laid for these people to be willing visitors again next year. In fact, this meeting might well be the time for them to fill out a brief evaluation of the experience and indicate if they are willing to serve as visitors again in the future.

While the preparation phase of the annual commitment drive may extend over many weeks or months, the invitation phase should be very brief. Normally churches find it effective to designate one Sunday to kick off the drive publicly and to make as many visits as possible. The following week can be used for visitors to call on those not reached. Those not reached within that time period should not be forgotten, but should be contacted in another manner.

For those who cannot be visited personally, for whatever reason, the next best approach is the telephone. "Current results indicate that, on the average, telephone solicitation will be ten to twenty times more effective than a good direct-mail appeal. It is personal and permits all-important two-way communication."[13] In much the same way that visitors are trained, callers can be trained to phone those not personally visited.

For those who cannot be visited in person or by phone, an invitation to respond should be made by letter. Again, the more personal the letter is, the better the response will be. First-class, hand-stamped, hand-addressed envelopes convey personalization. The letter itself should likewise reflect individual attention. With today's word processing equipment there is no reason to send an impersonal letter for this once-a-year commitment.

66

4. *Celebration*. Once most of the commitments are received, which should be a week or two after beginning, the attained goal should be announced and celebrated in a worship service. The service could be developed around the theme of thanksgiving. Because an annual commitment drive often is scheduled to conclude around the Thanksgiving season, this theme would fit well in the church calendar. A litany of thanks could be prepared especially for the occasion, celebrating the attained goal and the opportunity it represents to be faithful witnesses to God. Through the litany and prayers and hymns, the community could be led to acknowledge that "we give thee but thine own, whate'er the gift may be; all that we have is thine alone, a trust, O Lord, from thee."[14]

5. *Evaluation*. The annual commitment drive is not complete until the leaders come together to evaluate what worked well and what did not and what should be tried again and what should not. The evaluation should be written and preserved for whoever will be responsible for preparing the following year's drive. Include with this evaluation the names of those who are willing to be visitors again, along with any suggestions they have for improving the process.

In addition to giving proper attention to each of these steps, attention to several other items also can help ensure the success of a commitment drive. One is to stress tithing and percentage giving in all communications related to the drive. This emphasis appropriately focuses the discussion of resources on biblical and theological reasons for giving rather than on church budget reasons for giving. A mention of tithing and percentage giving also encourages higher standards of giving than many persons currently practice. In this regard, showing graphs is often helpful in indicating what it would mean to give 1 percent, 2 percent, 5 percent, 10 percent, 12 percent, and so forth, of various levels of income each week.

Another item to consider is building a "ladder" which depicts weekly church giving by ranges. For example, how many giving units give between one dollar and ten dollars a week, how many between eleven dollars and twenty-five dollars, how many between twenty-six dollars and fifty dollars, and so forth? Quite often, people are surprised to learn they are not at the top in their giving and they are motivated to move up the ladder.

Third, church leaders should consider varying their approach from year to year. Any approach, no matter how well done, loses its effectiveness if repeated yearly. While the basic steps of preparation, education, invitation, celebration, and evaluation always will be necessary, church leaders should be continually on the lookout for creative annual commitment programs which enable them to tell their story and invite response in challenging new ways.

When the annual commitment drive is over, the work begins! The first task is to thank those who provided leadership. Some churches host special dinners for leaders and volunteers. While an appreciation dinner is most appropriate, key leaders should also be thanked in individual ways. Expressing appreciation individually may mean a personal visit from the pastor to say thanks to the chairpersons of various committees and phone calls to others. Notes from chairpersons to committee members are not quickly forgotten and let volunteers know their efforts were appreciated.

The next task is to thank those who made commitments. Again, those who made outstanding commitments need to be thanked personally. A visit from the pastor to express appreciation on behalf of the church and to let persons know how important their commitments are is always appropriate. And every commitment, no matter what the size, should receive a written acknowledgment.

Because churches don't usually send out thank-you letters for weekly offerings, ways also should be found to thank people on a regular basis for their gifts. Acknowledgment of their support during pastoral visits, words of appreciation in church bulletins and newsletters, and occasional notes of thanks are all possibilities.

The key is to thank people immediately for their commitment and regularly for their gifts. One fund raiser suggests that when persons make a gift, they should be thanked until they make the next one. Certainly the possibility for future gifts is greater when one is appropriately thanked. Chuck Allen tells the true story of visiting a retired woman and thanking her for her two dollar gift. She was so impressed that she later gave thirty-nine thousand dollars.[15]

The third task is to make sure that persons can make gifts and fulfill their commitment easily. A church can assist people in making their gifts in a number of ways. An obvious way is to make sure the offering envelopes are large enough to receive checks or paper money easily and not just coins. A less obvious way to assist gift givers is to provide

68

self-addressed business reply envelopes so gifts can be mailed to the church.

Church leaders also should inform members that noncash gifts are acceptable. A tragic but true story is told of a man who made a substantial gift of securities to another organization after church leaders told him they were unprepared to accept such a gift. Church leaders should know how to accept gifts of securities, insurance, and property, and they should publicize that such gifts are welcome.

A fourth task is to keep people informed about what their gifts are accomplishing. Through articles in the church newsletter, announcements at church, and personal conversations, people should know that their gifts are being put to good use and are helping to undergird existing programs and establish new outreach ministries.

Finally, people need to be kept informed about how the church is doing toward its goals and how they are personally doing toward theirs. Gift amounts received toward the church budget can be noted regularly (either weekly or monthly) in the church bulletin or newsletter. Individuals should likewise be informed regularly (quarterly or semi-annually) about the status of their own pledge commitments.

The purpose of carrying out these tasks after the annual commitment drive is to help ensure that commitments are fulfilled and church goals are met.

Developing an effective annual giving program is not something that can be accomplished in a matter of weeks, but is a continuous cycle which begins with stewardship education, develops into an invitation to respond, and matures into strong annual support through sustained demonstrations of appreciation and accountability. Developing such a program requires effort, perseverance, and patience. Establishing an annual giving program is an important goal for church leaders, as an effective annual giving program provides the necessary foundation for a strong church.

TO SUMMARIZE

The first step in developing an effective annual giving program is to create a strong year-round stewardship education program. The purpose of this program is to inform, inspire, and challenge congregational members regarding their stewardship commitment. The program should permeate all areas of church life, including worship, Christian education, and the various organizations within the church. In addition to the existing programs of the church, periodic study groups and covenant/prayer groups might also be created for the specific purpose of growing in stewardship understanding and commitment.

The second step is to invite a response through an annual commitment drive. A successful commitment drive focuses on biblical reasons for giving rather than on the church budget. Such a drive involves five steps: preparation, education, invitation, celebration, and evaluation. The invitation to respond should always be as personal as possible, with a goal being to visit as many people as possible face-to-face. The telephone is the second choice for inviting people to respond, and a personal letter is the third choice.

The third step in developing an effective annual giving program is to demonstrate appreciation and accountability. Appreciation can be expressed by thanking members immediately for their commitment and regularly thereafter for gifts received. Accountability can be demonstrated by keeping members informed about what their gifts are accomplishing, what the status of the church budget is, and what the status of their own commitment is.

Developing an effective annual giving program is a long-term endeavor. One pastor referred to it as a twenty-year program.

Chapter Six

DEVELOPING AN EFFECTIVE CAPITAL GIVING PROGRAM

"A capital campaign is a concentrated effort by an organization or institution to raise a specified *sum of money to meet a* specified *goal within a* specified *period of time."*

Thomas E. Broce[1]

Broce's definition of a capital campaign is a tightly packed one. Let's unpack it piece by piece.

"Concentrated effort" means that the leadership of the church (staff and volunteers) will need to devote significant amounts of time and energy to this endeavor. The involvement and teamwork of a large number of people working together will be required.

"Specified sum of money" indicates that there is a clearly defined financial goal. Raising this amount is essential if the organizational goal is to be accomplished.

"Specified goal" suggests that the church has engaged in long-range planning. From this planning, specific organizational goals have emerged to address well-defined needs.

"Specified period of time" implies deadlines. There is some urgency to raise this money within those deadlines so that the organizational goal can be accomplished.

Capital gifts are gifts received for specific projects over and above the annual giving budget. Oftentimes the projects are related to facilities, such as a new building or an addition or renovation of an existing building. Capital gifts can also be received for programs. Such gifts might be invited, for example, to underwrite a new mission outreach program or to endow an existing scholarship program. Capital gifts most frequently are solicited during a "campaign," that intensive time described in Broce's definition above.

Capital giving is thus the second major component in a well-designed giving program within a church. Capital gifts allow a church to address goals beyond the scope of the annual budget which emerge through long-range planning, and to maintain adequate facilities for worship, programming, and outreach. The purpose of this chapter is to help church leaders develop an effective capital giving program.

The importance of a capital giving program should not be overlooked. A large percentage—some suggest 90 percent or more—of total gifts received by charitable organizations is received in the form of special and major gifts for designated projects. Persons make major gifts to capital projects much more readily than they do to the annual budget because capital projects often have high price tags and also because capital gifts are frequently seen as more enduring. Persons find satisfaction in making major gifts that will have a lasting impact. Helping to build buildings, create endowments, and establish other major programs offers this kind of satisfaction to many.

In every church are members who could give significantly more than they give to the annual budget, but who will not be motivated to make larger gifts simply to fund current operation. If the church does not capture their attention with programs and projects of significant importance, then quite possibly their major gifts will go to other charitable institutions.

Churches should not embark on capital giving programs simply to receive major gifts, but church leaders must think creatively and plan boldly, recognizing that some people are looking for opportunities to invest themselves and their resources. One woman put it well when she stated: "As we get older or see the end of an era, we give more thought to leaving a mark in the world. 'What difference will it make that I lived?' becomes an important question." The church has the responsibility to offer opportunities that will make a difference and to strengthen the church's mission through a capital giving program.

What are the opportunities churches can offer? The possibilities are endless, limited only by a congregation's imagination. While building projects have been at the forefront of capital campaigns for years, many other projects and programs offer marvelous opportunities to expand a church's vision and outreach. Some churches, for example, have worked toward the goal of spending a dollar externally for every dollar spent internally. Thus, for every dollar spent within the church —for heat, lights, salaries, or whatever—another dollar is raised to assist church-related institutions, to sponsor a missionary, or to support some other outreach program.

Some churches recognize the importance of preparing future leaders for the church and, therefore, become partners with seminaries in training such leaders by creating endowed scholarships. Other churches recognize the importance of Christian camping experiences for youth, so they establish permanent funds to assist in sending their youth to camp each year. Some churches develop sister relationships with churches in third world countries and provide resources for those churches to strengthen their own programs and outreach ministries. Capital giving programs can assist in these and countless other undertakings, as donors are invited to underwrite such endeavors with major gifts over and above their annual support to the church.

A capital giving program should not be entered into hastily, however. Because annual giving needs will continue in the midst of a capital campaign, a church should not embark on a capital giving program until a sound and well-supported annual giving program is in place. Also, because most capital programs are intensive efforts which are dependent upon major gift support in order to be successful, it is critical that the programs be well-planned and coordinated.

The impetus for a capital giving program should be the church's long-range plan. If the planning committee is doing its work in a thoughtful and creative manner, it should be identifying a number of long-range dreams, goals, and opportunities to be addressed. The dollars needed to bring about these dreams and goals form the basis for a capital giving program.

The essential elements of fund raising, outlined in Chapter 3, are as important in a capital giving program as they are in annual giving and should be reviewed before embarking on any major effort. In addition to these elements, professional fund raising counsel suggests the following six distinct phases in a capital campaign:[2]

1. Planning	4. General solicitation
2. Organization	5. Celebration
3. Major gift solicitation	6. Transition

Let us look at each phase.

1. *Planning.* The first step in the planning phase is to review the organizational goals in the long-range plan. Which goals have the

highest priority? Which goals have the greatest urgency? Those goals with both high priority and urgency should become the campaign goals. Identify several goals so that the campaign will have broad appeal to a large number of people. Repairing the church organ may have great urgency and be a high priority, and it may be the most important project to be addressed at this time. Rather than making it the only item in a campaign, however, a church would do well to include some other goals along with this one. Not everyone will be interested in the organ project. If the church also includes in the campaign some additional goals from its long-range plan, the likelihood is that these too will be funded, and the campaign will have broader appeal.

Another important part of the planning phase is to determine whether or not to use professional counsel. If the campaign goal is less than $100,000, if there is campaign experience in the present leadership, and if there is flexibility in the timeline for raising the money, the church may opt to conduct the campaign without professional counsel. On the other hand, if it is the first time for a capital campaign under present leadership, if the campaign has some urgency, or if the dollar goal is $100,000 or more, professional counsel is recommended.

Professional consultants are never inexpensive, but this should not be the determining factor in whether or not to use their expertise. Too often churches are penny-wise and pound-foolish, saving money in the beginning by not hiring professional counsel, only to fall short of their campaign goals in the end. Harold Seymour reminds us that "you can't raise money without spending money, and within reasonable limits the return is likely to be commensurate with the investment."[3] Dollars invested in professional counsel are well spent if they enable the church to reach its goals.

Of course, hiring professional counsel does not guarantee that a campaign will be successful. However, the likelihood for success is much greater, for professionals bring with them expertise and experience from many previous campaigns.

Professional consultants can be helpful in a variety of ways. Consultants can be especially valuable in helping to set and test the financial goals, create a campaign plan and timetable, train staff and volunteers, and supervise the overall campaign effort. Professional consultants can provide services at practically any level desired, from full-time cam-

74

paign direction to part-time counsel on a retainer basis. Most professional consultants are quite willing to meet with organizations to outline their services and suggest options for consideration.

Church leaders considering professional counsel might want to interview one or more firms. A good place to begin looking is at denominational headquarters. Many denominations employ professional fund raising consultants for the very purpose of assisting local churches in their campaigns. A plus they bring is familiarity with the church structure. Church leaders also might want to consider consulting firms in their community which have a good track record. In interviewing potential consultants, church leaders should look for firms which are sensitive to their particular situation and are willing to be flexible.

Today a majority of institutions use professional fund raising counsel when they embark on a capital campaign. Most churches would be well served if they did likewise. Even in a relatively small campaign, employing professional counsel on a limited basis at the beginning would help ensure that the campaign is appropriately organized with realistic goals and timetables.

Noted fund raiser Arthur Frantzreb suggests answering three important questions before going much further in planning:

> 1. Is there a real need to conduct this campaign, and, if so, is there some urgency about it, or does the governing board believe that the campaign could be deferred until later?
> 2. Are there now enough prospects with enough potential to whom this campaign can be addressed?
> 3. Are there enough volunteers on the governing board to lead the campaign and help assure its success?[4]

Positive answers to the above questions indicate that the church is in a good position to launch a capital campaign. Negative responses to any of the above may indicate that the timing or the goals of the campaign should be rethought before proceeding further. Some uncertainty always accompanies launching a campaign, of course, and a church should not wait until it is 100 percent certain of success in order to begin. Such certainty only means that the goal is probably too modest! If a majority of the leadership responds negatively to more than one of the above questions, however, the church should proceed cautiously, if at all. After all, this group is who will determine the

75

success of any campaign, and they must be enthusiastic and positive about the goals and the likelihood of success.

2. *Organization.* Once church leaders are prepared to move ahead with a capital campaign, organizing for it should begin. If professional consultants are to be used, bring them in at this point as they can be most helpful in the organizational phase.

An important task in this phase is to determine a tentative fund raising goal, and to test out the reasonableness of this goal. Prepare a projected gift table which indicates the number of gifts needed at various levels. In preparing such a table, plan that anywhere from 10 to 20 percent of the goal should come from one donor. The gift table is then completed by doubling the donors and halving the gifts. For example, a capital campaign goal of $230,000 would have a gift table similar to the following:

1 gift at	$30,000	= $30,000
2 gifts at	$15,000	= $30,000
4 gifts at	$ 7,500	= $30,000
10 gifts at	$ 3,000	= $30,000
20 gifts at	$ 1,500	= $30,000
40 gifts at	$ 1,000	= $40,000
Many gifts under	$ 1,000	= $40,000
Total		$230,000

Once such a table is prepared, it should be revised as necessary, based on the number of potential donors and the reasonableness of the dollar figures at both ends of the table. For example, if a church has a small donor base and it is improbable that $40,000 would be received in many small commitments under $1,000, the table would need to be adjusted upward.

The campaign goals then can be tested by sharing a draft of the case statement and the projected gift table with a number of key persons for their input. These persons should be asked to comment on the appropriateness of the goals, to identify those who might be leaders in supporting the campaign, and to indicate their own level of support on the gift table.

Such a testing of the goals should give church leaders a good reading on the level of potential interest in and support for the campaign. Two other "tests" used by professional consultants are also helpful in assessing the campaign goal. One is to seek to identify at least four names for every gift needed at the various giving levels. If such names cannot be identified, it suggests the prospect base is too small and the likelihood of receiving the appropriate number of gifts at that level is reduced. The other "test" is to rate all prospective donors and then plan for only half of the prospects to give and at half the level they are capable of giving.

Engaging in these tests will add a note of reality to the campaign goal and may suggest revision. Leaders may discover that the goal is too modest and that other long-range goals also should be addressed in this campaign. Or they may discover that the goal needs to be adjusted downward. A challenging but realistic goal is far better than one which has little possibility of being reached. Whatever the outcome, the testing of goals will assist in preparing and organizing for the campaign.

Once the campaign goal has been tested and revised as necessary, a fund raising plan should be developed. A campaign steering committee, composed of six to twelve key leaders, should be recruited to coordinate the campaign. The committee's responsibilities will include developing the fund raising plan, determining campaign policies, soliciting major gifts, providing overall management of the campaign, and appointing other committees as needed. This committee will be critically important to the success of the campaign, and persons should be chosen who are capable and enthusiastic supporters and workers.

The fund raising plan will need to address such questions as the following: How will the annual commitment drive be handled during the campaign? What special events will be held to inform and inspire persons? How many volunteers will be needed and how will they be recruited and trained? What other committees will be needed to make this campaign effective? What will the campaign timetable look like? No simple answers to these questions can be given because they depend upon the size and makeup of the church and the campaign goal. However, in any situation, keep the organizational structure as streamlined as possible and at the same time involve as many people as possible in the work of the campaign. These two goals can be accomplished by keeping the number of campaign committees to a minimum and involving volunteers in a variety of short-term projects throughout the campaign. To mention just a few possibilities, volunteers will be needed to help prepare publicity, plan a kickoff event, and serve as solicitors.

The campaign timetable deserves particular attention in the fund raising plan. A timetable is necessary to keep the campaign progressing toward its goal in a timely fashion. Dates for completing certain phases of the campaign should be noted. Completion dates should be set for when the major gift solicitation will take place, when the public announcement will be held, when general solicitation will begin, and, most important, when the campaign will conclude. Professional fund raisers agree that a completion date for a campaign is vitally important, providing the necessary urgency to bring a campaign to a successful conclusion.

Again, timetables vary considerably depending upon local situations. However, it is unusual for a church to gear up for a capital campaign in less than a year. Conducting the campaign may take another year or two. Actual receipt of gifts is often spread out over a three- or five-year period. Offering a long pledge period allows persons to make much larger commitments than would be possible in a single gift. Longer pledge periods are not recommended, however, as new goals emerge which need addressing and church leadership may change.

Campaign policies that will need to be determined by the steering committee include such items as whether planned gift commitments will count toward the goal and what noncash gifts, such as securities and personal property, will be accepted. Other policies may need to be determined as special situations arise.

A final task in the organization phase is to prepare the campaign materials. Many capital campaigns are developed around a theme, and all campaign pieces, including stationery, pledge cards, and brochures, display this theme. Planning around a theme can be an effective way to reinforce the importance of the campaign. Once again the most important campaign piece will be the case statement, and particular care should be devoted to making sure it is professionally and attractively prepared. Regarding campaign materials, Broce quotes an important maxim, "Few people give money, because of publicity, but fewer give without it."[5] Developing campaign materials which can inform and inspire is important; however, these materials will not win the campaign by themselves. Spending too much money on materials can have a negative effect on campaigns by wasting money and turning people off. Thus, in preparing materials an appropriate balance should be sought.

3. *Major gift solicitation.* Major gift solicitation should begin before the campaign is publicly announced. Major gifts will continue to be sought throughout the duration of the campaign, but it is vitally important to seek and receive some major gift commitments before the campaign ever officially begins. These gifts will set the pace for the campaign and will raise the sights of others who will be invited to give once the campaign is officially launched.

The importance of major gift solicitation can be understood when one realizes that the success or failure of a campaign often depends upon one or two major gifts. As noted earlier, it is not uncommon for one or two gifts to account for 20 percent of a campaign goal. Harold Seymour refers to the rule of three, which suggests "about one-third of the money has to come from the top ten gifts, another third from the next 100 gifts, and the last third from all other gifts."[6] This rule has proved to be amazingly accurate in a variety of situations, and again it underscores the importance of major gifts for the success of any campaign.

Professional fund raisers suggest the proper approach in soliciting major gifts is "top down, inside out." This phrase means that you begin soliciting those who are the top prospects for major gifts (the top ten) and work down (focusing on the next one hundred prospects, and then on the rest). At the same time, you begin soliciting those who are closest to and most involved in the life of the church and work your way out to those who are least involved. The top prospects will thus be those who have major gift potential and who are also deeply involved in the life of the church. A number of the major gift prospects should be on the campaign steering committee because this group is most deeply involved in the success of the campaign and will be soliciting other major givers.

Major gift prospects should be visited personally. The first visits can be made by the senior pastor and the chairperson of the steering committee (after they have made their own commitments, of course) to other steering committee members. Once steering committee members have made their commitments, they can begin visiting others. Solicitors should visit those who have similar interests and who can make commitments in a range comparable to their own.

"To strongly urge (as one's cause)" is a definition for the word *solicit,* and this aptly describes the solicitor's responsibility. Persons calling on others should be prepared to discuss why they believe this

79

campaign is important and to urge support for it. They should share enthusiastically why they are investing their time and money in this effort, and they should be prepared to indicate the level of their financial commitment. In so doing, they demonstrate the depth of their commitment and invite by example.

These persons who visit should also be prepared to share the range of gifts needed (a copy of the gift table is a handy resource at this point) and to indicate what they hope the person will consider giving (this amount is determined by the steering committee, or persons it appoints, when the prospect rating is done in the organization phase). The latter is most important because people want and need to know what is expected of them. If done in a gracious way, people will welcome this word. John D. Rockefeller, Jr., delivered a talk in 1933 which highlights this truth.

> Another suggestion I like to have made me by a solicitor is how much it is hoped I will give. Of course, such a suggestion can be made in a way that might be most annoying. I do not like to have anyone tell me what it is my duty to give. There is just one man who is going to decide that question, who has the responsibility of deciding it, and that is myself. But I do like a man to say to me, "We are trying to raise $4,000,000 and are hoping you may be desirous of giving (blank) dollars. If you see your way clear to do so, it will be an enormous help and encouragement. You may have it in mind to give more; if so, we will be glad. On the other hand, you may feel you cannot give as much, in view of other responsibilities. If that is the case, we shall understand. Whatever you give after thinking the matter over carefully in the light of the need, your other obligations, and your desire to do your full share as a citizen, will be gratefully received and deeply appreciated.[7]

Naming opportunities are sometimes attractive to major donors. Include such opportunities in a campaign and describe these opportunities at the time that persons are asked to consider a gift. Persons can be inspired to make larger commitments than planned if they see an attractive opportunity to honor a loved one or preserve the family name through a gift.

Finally, solicitors should be prepared to discuss giving methods, informing the prospect that pledges can be spread out over (x) number of years and that in addition to cash, commitments can be fulfilled through gifts of securities and real estate or planned gift arrangements (if indeed the church is prepared to accept such gifts). If a prospect is not prepared to make a decision, the pledge card should not be left. Instead, an appointment should be made for a follow-up visit in a few days. In a second visit, the importance of the campaign can again be stressed, any questions can be answered, and a pledge can be received.

4. *General solicitation.* A good share of the work is done before a campaign is ever officially launched. Indeed, many fund raising consultants suggest that 40 to 50 percent of the goal should be pledged before publicly announcing a campaign. This early pledge amount allows the campaign to be launched on a very positive note and also enables the public phase of the campaign to be conducted at a rather brisk pace.

Campaigns are often set in motion with kickoff events. A kickoff event needs to be planned and orchestrated carefully so that people leave with excitement and expectation. The whole congregation should be invited to this affair. Balloons, banners, and brochures can be used to help create a festive atmosphere. However, the key to the event's success will be the spoken words of individuals. The pastor should set the tone with an impassioned presentation about how achieving the campaign goals can enrich the church and its ministries. The case can be presented by the chairperson of the steering committee. This presentation might be followed by several short endorsements from key leaders who have made substantial commitments and who can speak with warmth and intensity about why the campaign is deserving of each member's generous support. The event's finale should be the announcement of the campaign total achieved up to that date.

General solicitation of members should follow soon after the kickoff event while enthusiasm is still high. The same principles used in major gift solicitation apply here, with individuals being personally visited wherever possible and invited to consider a gift level recommended by the steering committee. Additional solicitors can be recruited from the ranks of those who already have made commitments. They should be carefully chosen because of their own strong commitment and their ability to inspire commitment in others. Enough solicitors should be recruited so that no individual needs to call on more than five prospects.

The challenge in the general solicitation phase is to sustain the momentum of the campaign. Unless the solicitation is completed fairly

81

soon after the kickoff event, enthusiasm probably will begin to wane. Regular communication and publicity should be a top priority for the steering committee during this phase in order to keep the importance and urgency of the campaign alive. A campaign newsletter can be especially effective. It can restate the importance of the campaign goals, announce the pledge totals, report news of important developments, feature personal testimonies, and pay tribute to volunteers. A crisp, cheery newsletter distributed on a regular basis can play an important role in moving the campaign along.

The challenge gift is another effective means of keeping the campaign moving. One or more individuals make a pledge that is dependent upon additional gifts being received within a certain time period. For example, a challenge might be to match all gifts received dollar for dollar, up to a certain limit by a specified date. Or a challenge might be to complete the campaign with a gift of (x) dollars if the remainder can be pledged by the time the campaign is to conclude. The challenge gift can be attractive to those who like to increase the impact of their own gift and provide the necessary impetus for others to respond. A challenge gift made toward the end of the campaign can be especially helpful in motivating those who have not yet responded to act before the deadline. It can even encourage additional gifts from those who have responded earlier. The steering committee may wish to invite a major donor to consider a challenge gift, or the committee members collectively may decide to offer such a gift themselves.

In spite of the best efforts to invite responses by the campaign deadline, there will be some, for a variety of reasons, who have not made commitments. Depending upon how close they are to achieving the goal, the members of the steering committee may decide to extend the campaign deadline or to honor the deadline but continue to work quietly with those who realistically can be expected to make a commitment.

5. *Celebration.* An important function of the church is to recognize and celebrate significant landmarks in the lives of individuals and the congregation as a whole. Individual landmarks that are recognized and celebrated include birth, marriage, and death, as well as other important occasions. Corporate landmarks include church anniversaries and special holy days within the Christian calendar.

The successful conclusion of a capital campaign in the life of a church is also worthy of appropriate celebration. Such a celebration should include the dimension of worship, for worship at its best is celebration, and celebration at its best is worship. The worship should focus on praise and thanks to God for providing the vision for new areas of growth and ministry, and for providing the resources to enable the congregation to respond to this vision. The worship celebration places the whole campaign in an appropriate context by reminding the community of faith that all gifts come from God and are to be dedicated for the purpose of carrying out God's will.

In addition to offering thanks to God in worship, a celebration should provide opportunity to offer thanks to those who gave unstintingly of their time and talents to help assure the campaign's success. In an atmosphere of fun and fellowship, perhaps at a congregational meal following a celebrative worship service, persons who played key leadership roles in the campaign should be recognized and thanked. In addition to words of appreciation, appropriate mementoes, perhaps relating to the campaign theme, could also be presented to those who provided outstanding leadership.

Finally, a celebration should provide opportunity for the entire community of faith to be thanked and to rejoice together in this achievement of goals. The message to be communicated in this part of the celebration is that the goal was achieved because of the combined efforts of many and that every gift was important. Thus, the celebration could end as a party with everyone being feted and recognized as an important member of the Body of Christ.

6. *Transition.* While the afterglow of the victory celebration still lingers, church leaders should begin the transition phase. The first step is to meet and do a complete evaluation of the campaign. This evaluation should include a review of campaign materials, events, committees, timetable, and any other important areas unique to that particular campaign. In each area of concern, that which worked well and that which did not should be noted. Because capital campaigns are only occasional events, this evaluation should be written and preserved for the future.

Preparing a record of the campaign is equally important, and the record should be as complete as possible. In addition to the written evaluation and samples of campaign materials, the record should include copies of the following: original goals and actual results, comparison of the gift table to actual commitments received, minutes from committee meetings, a final budget report on campaign expenses, campaign policies statement, projected and actual time-tables, and a list of all pledges and all campaign reports. Although such information should be readily available and therefore relatively easy to put together, many organizations forget to do so once a campaign is over. This record should be preserved as a reference for future campaigns, and there will be future campaigns!

Because capital campaigns frequently involve multi-year pledges, another important transition step is to ensure that pledges are properly recorded and that a system is set up to send out periodic reminders. Again, neglect of this step can end a successful campaign with a disastrous conclusion.

A final transition step is to begin identifying other projects and programs worthy of capital support. The church should not immediately begin another capital campaign; the church should not even consider one for at least three to five years because pledges to this campaign need to be completed before another campaign is launched. In between major campaigns, however, a church can lift up additional projects and programs which do not require the intensity of a campaign but nonetheless invite capital support. Some who have had their sights raised during a campaign will welcome these opportunities to respond. If the planning committee continues to do its work on a regular basis, a ready list of dreams, goals, and opportunities for capital investment should always be available.

One can only wonder what might have happened to George Bidwell and Friendship Church (described in Chapter 1) if they had given careful attention to each of these campaign phases in their effort to raise money for a new church addition. One can hope that they, and many others, will plan a campaign again in the future and incorporate these phases into their plan, for a well-planned and well-executed capital campaign provides a church with many benefits.

1. It enhances the visibility of the mission and programs of the church and provides an opportunity to lift up important priorities.
2. It allows the church to address important long-range goals.
3. It expands the horizons of church members and helps them to grow in their stewardship commitment.

4. It provides opportunities for persons to make major gifts for the work of the church which they might otherwise not make toward the annual budget.
5. It broadens the support base of the church and often brings about a new level of support to the annual budget.
6. It enables the church to enlist and involve new volunteers and train new leadership for the church.

The benefits of an effective capital giving program thus go far beyond dollars received, and church leaders seriously should consider occasional capital campaigns as a part of a well-developed stewardship emphasis.

TO SUMMARIZE

Capital giving is the second major component in a well-designed giving program. Capital gifts are received for specific projects and programs which grow out of long-range planning, but are beyond the scope of the annual budget. Capital gifts generally are received during an intensive campaign, although they can be made at any time.

A capital campaign should be launched only when an annual giving program is well established. Because a campaign involves a significant commitment of time and energy from church leaders, it should be launched only if there are genuine and urgent goals, enthusiastic and positive support for the goals, and a willingness on the part of church leaders to invest themselves in the campaign.

A capital campaign is composed of six separate phases, all of which are vitally important. The phases are planning, organization, major gift solicitation, general solicitation, celebration, and transition.

In addition to providing funds to meet major long-range goals, a capital campaign provides new opportunities for involvement and leadership in the church, challenges individuals to grow in their stewardship commitment, and enhances the visibility of the church's programs and priorities.

Chapter Seven

DEVELOPING AN EFFECTIVE PLANNED GIVING PROGRAM

"Perhaps nothing in local church programming is so neglected as stewardship in the area of deferred giving."

Raymond B. Knudsen[1]

Planned giving is the third major component in a well-designed giving program. *Planned giving* is a term used to describe giving through annuities, bequests, life insurance, real estate, and trusts. "These gifts are known as deferred gifts, and *planned giving* is often synonymous with *deferred giving.*"[2] Planned giving also includes current giving arrangements which require legal or tax planning. However, deferred gifts usually comprise the bulk of a planned giving program.

This third giving component generally receives the least attention by most church leaders; in many cases, it receives no attention at all. The results of such inattention are astounding. Giving through one's will is the most common type of deferred gift. Yet, "more than one of every two Americans dies without a will."[3] Of those who do have wills, "73.6 percent of the clergy and 84.6 percent of the laity have not included a bequest to their church."[4]

Why is this such a neglected area in church giving programs? Many churches find they have to focus so much time and attention on meeting the annual budget and conducting occasional capital campaigns that little enthusiasm is shown for considering a planned giving program.

Also, many churches do not engage in long-range planning, but focus instead on the immediate future. Planned giving is not seen as a viable solution to short-term needs. Because planned gift income seems like such a distant possibility, it rarely receives priority attention.

Some church leaders regard planned giving as an option only for the wealthy. These leaders think that a planned giving program would have little appeal in their congregation; therefore, they see no need to promote it.

Some church leaders simply feel embarrassed or uncomfortable in suggesting that the church should encourage planned gifts. "We are always asking for money from people when they are alive; must we also ask for a gift when they die?" is a question which has been raised more than once.

The fact of the matter, however, is that none of these are legitimate reasons for neglecting a planned giving program. Church leaders are terribly short-sighted not to have a planned giving program in place and to promote it regularly. The benefits of such a program are many.

1. Planned giving provides a tremendous opportunity for Christians to make a powerful witness to their faith and their values. Those who have been faithful in their giving throughout their lifetime can continue to make a witness at the time of death. Douglas Johnson puts it well when he states, "A Christian does not allow a giving life pattern to end suddenly because his or her heart stops beating."[5] Yet the contributions of many Christians do stop simply because they have not been encouraged to regard planned giving as another opportunity to make a witness. An elderly woman who had been a tither all her life was once asked if she had ever considered tithing her estate. Her response was no; then disappointment covered her face as she asked, "How come no pastor ever suggested that to me?" One wonders how many other Christians may feel similarly cheated.

2. Planned giving also helps maintain the work of the church and its related institutions. A gift from an individual's estate to a church's endowment or trust fund is a gift that will keep on giving in perpetuity, helping to assure the continued strength and vitality of its ministries. What could bring greater satisfaction than knowing our resources are continuing to positively influence and benefit others even when we are no longer here?

3. Planned giving enables persons to make larger charitable gifts than otherwise possible. Most annual gifts come from current income. Planned gifts, however, can come from one's accumulated assets when they are no longer needed. Through planned giving, persons often can

make larger gifts than they ever dreamed possible to those institutions that are important to them.

4. Planned giving allows persons to establish permanent living memorials for themselves or others. Few remembrances are as lasting, or as meaningful, as a living memorial which continues to minister to others in Christ's name for generations to come. Scholarship funds, lecture funds, and funds for missionary support are just a few types of living memorials that have been created through planned gifts.

5. Planned giving also provides tax advantages for the donor. In addition to charitable deductions, many planned gift arrangements provide the opportunity to reduce estate taxes and receive lifetime income. Some arrangements enable persons to increase their own spendable income at the same time that they make a planned gift.

6. Planned giving enhances both annual and capital giving programs. When persons make planned gift commitments to an institution, their interest and involvement in that institution often increase, as does their annual support. Likewise, capital giving programs are often significantly enhanced through planned gift arrangements. Individuals wishing to make a major commitment to a capital giving program frequently discover they can best do so· through a combination of outright gifts and planned gifts.

The fact is that planned gifts are a very important source of revenue for charitable institutions. Studies indicate, for example, that almost one-third of total individual giving to educational institutions consistently comes from planned gifts.[6] Bequest giving to nonprofit organizations reached an estimated $5.98 billion in 1987, and that amount continues to increase each year.[7]

Religious organizations, however, are not receiving a large percentage of planned gifts. Whereas outright gifts to religious organizations far outweigh donations to any other type of charity, only 10 percent of planned gifts go to religion. Why don't churches receive a larger percentage? It's because most have not learned what educational institutions have known for a long time: A consistent planned giving program can produce significant dollars over time. Most institutions of higher education have planned giving programs of some kind. Thus, it should not be surprising that 70 percent of bequest dollars went to education in 1987.

Most churches, on the other hand, have neither planned giving programs nor planned giving policies in place and often don't consider either necessary until they find themselves the unexpected recipients of a planned gift. This, you may recall, is what happened to Community Church in Chapter 1. With no planned giving policy in place, the church found itself torn about how to handle this gift. Unfortunately, that situation is not uncommon.

Receiving sizable bequests would be more common, however, if churches had a well-defined planned giving program. Raymond Knudsen suggests that "often local churches do not receive sizable grants and bequests because, deep down, potential donors question the financial integrity of the organization. No church can afford this luxury."[8] Potential planned givers want and deserve assurance that their gifts will be well managed and will be used for the purpose intended. So many horror stories exist of mismanagement and improper use of funds that many will not consider a planned gift to a church, and properly so, unless the church has demonstrated a willingness to receive such gifts and an ability to manage them appropriately.

Thus, a planned giving program needs to be proactive, not reactive. The church that waits to receive its first planned gift before developing a policy is courting trouble—and perhaps a long wait! The church would be in a far better position to develop a policy and program which encouraged gifts for specific purposes. Like other giving programs, a planned giving program would then receive gifts for well-defined needs and ministries rather than gifts that might be inconsistent with a church's goals or no gifts at all.

Some church leaders shy away from encouraging planned gifts for fear that a large planned gift would discourage regular giving among church members. Indeed, if a church does not have a policy in place, then members sometimes think that the planned gift can replace their regular support. However, if the church has thoughtfully defined how planned gifts will be used, many members are led to make planned gift commitments and to increase their regular support.

In 1983 the United Methodist church in Ruthven, Iowa, learned that it was to receive a large sum of money from two estates. As one member noted, "It was very exciting but an awesome responsibility to use such an amount of money wisely, and do good and worthwhile things with it."[9] The church recognized the need to establish some guidelines immediately. Congregational members were invited to share their dreams and priorities. Even though the economic situation was not good, no consideration was given to using any of the money for the local church budget. The leaders recognized that using bequest money for the regular budget would mean the death of the church. Instead, they reached the consensus to use a portion of the funds for some immediate community needs and to invest the rest in a permanent fund. The leaders further determined that interest from this permanent fund would be used each year according to the following guidelines:

Special local church projects	30%
Community projects	25%
Conference programs and projects	10%
National and international projects	25%
Reinvestment	10%

That same year the church oversubscribed its annual budget. The pastor summarizes the importance of these planned gifts by stating: "We have become a stronger church through the process. Individually and as a body we have grown in our understanding of God and of His will for us in this area of stewardship." [10]

Wesley United Methodist Church in Macomb, Illinois, has a similar story to tell. In 1967 the members learned that the church would someday receive a significant bequest. The church trustees appointed an ad hoc committee to study and develop a plan for the proper management and use of this bequest. The committee spent considerable time developing a careful plan. Ultimately the committee recommended that a trust be established for the perpetuation of the bequest and that a trust committee of five members be appointed for five-year terms. The ad hoc committee further recommended that a bank serve as the trustee for this trust and that only the income be used for the Christian outreach of the church. Of the spendable portion, the trust agreement stipulated that 10 percent would be for the general and benevolent budgets of the local church ("the tithe paid to the church"), and the remaining 90 percent would be for religious and charitable grants outside the local church. [11]

In 1971 the trustees approved the adoption of this plan, and in 1973 the trust became fully operational when the church member died. Since that time the trust fund has given away more than five million dollars to more than a hundred different church-related, educational, and civic organizations. The pastor notes that the church was mission minded before the bequest was received, and the gift has enhanced the church's commitment to missions.

Two important similarities in these examples should be noted. First, in both cases policies were established which stipulated that the majority of funds were to be used for projects and programs external to the local church. Thus, church members were not tempted to cut back on their giving to the local church, but rather were challenged to grow in mission mindedness as the church reached out in new ministries.

In both churches the leaders regarded the planned gifts as opportunities to expand their stewardship, not lessen it. The pastor of Ruthven United Methodist Church indicates that the church's fund continues to remind people of the great number of mission projects deserving support. Similarly the pastor of Wesley United Methodist Church states that serving on the trust committee is a very important educational experience. As committee members review requests and decide which to fund, their vision of the world and their awareness of mission opportunities are increased.

Second, both churches decided to create permanent funds so these planned gifts could continue to serve others for generations to come. Some church leaders believe that churches should not have endowment funds and that such funds are a liability for a congregation's own stewardship. As the above examples indicate, however, the problem is not endowment funds per se, but how these funds are used. If policies are established for the use of endowment funds, an endowment can enhance the vision and the giving of a congregation.

Restrictions on an endowment fund should not be too narrowly defined, but should have enough flexibility to allow church leaders to respond to important priorities and needs. The two churches just described and many others have found that an appropriate way to establish guidelines and maintain flexibility is to create various categories of ministry and then determine a certain percentage of earnings which can be used for each category. As noted above, the one thing to avoid with endowment funds is to use them primarily to support the annual budgetary needs of the church. If endowment funds are to enhance the vision and ministry of a church, they should be used primarily as seed money to support new and creative ministries within the church or important ministries beyond the local church. Wesley United Methodist Church's decision to direct 90 percent of the trust earnings to external projects is an exemplary model which other churches would do well to follow. Such a model encourages churches to learn about and become partners with their denominational colleges and seminaries, their national and international mission offices, and other local, state, national, and international ministries.

A similar model for endowments which is popular among churches is to establish a few major funding categories and to invite persons to make designated gifts to any of the categories. Categories might include the following:

Mission fund. Gifts contributed to this fund would be used for mission activities in the community and beyond.

Building fund. Gifts made to this fund would be used for the repair, renovation, or construction of church facilities and for grounds improvements.

General fund. Undesignated gifts could be placed in this fund as well as gifts designated especially for this area. This fund would provide the greatest flexibility and would allow a governing board to direct funds to those programs and ministries consistent with the church's mission and primary goals.

Endowments are the lifeblood of many charitable institutions, providing the necessary financial stability to address the future creatively. Churches considering a planned giving program should at the same time consider the possibility of establishing an endowment fund, for endowments and planned giving programs complement one another very well. Although planned gifts do not have to be placed in endowments, doing so is appealing because donors then know that their gifts will have a lasting influence, assisting in the ministry of the church for generations to come.

Because planned gifts are the major way that endowments are built, churches sometimes establish an endowment fund at the same time that they launch a planned giving program. A brochure then can be prepared which describes the endowment fund and the planned giving program and invites congregational support. This brochure helps stimulate interest in planned giving and enables members to see how such gifts will benefit the long-term goals of the church.

If an endowment fund is created, a written policy should be prepared indicating how the fund will be invested and managed and how income will be disbursed. Ruthven United Methodist Church wisely chose to reinvest some of its earnings each year in order that their fund might continue to grow and keep pace with inflation. Some churches choose to manage their own funds; many others choose to have a denominational foundation or a bank invest, manage, and disburse funds according to guidelines prepared by the church. Many endowment funds have been created with a single significant planned gift. The likelihood of receiving such a gift is greatly enhanced if church members know a well-written policy is in place.

If a church chooses not to create an endowment fund, planned gifts should still be encouraged. Such gifts can be used to support capital projects, to launch new programs within the church, or to support ministry programs and projects outside the local church. Such gifts also can be directed to church-related institutions or denominational foundations for support of their work.

How does a church develop an effective planned giving program? Once again, several steps can be outlined:

1. Obtain approval
2. Appoint committee
3. Become informed
4. Prepare brochure
5. Develop policies
6. Promote and educate
7. Provide recognition

Let us look at each step.

1. *Obtain approval.* Church leaders first should seek the approval of the governing board to launch a planned giving program. The benefits of such a program, as outlined at the beginning of this chapter, should be presented and a commitment sought to support such a program for a minimum of three years. A three-year commitment is important; planned giving experts suggest it normally takes at least this long for an effective planned giving program to begin bearing fruit.

2. *Appoint committee.* Once the governing board has made a commitment to launch a planned giving program, a committee should be appointed to coordinate this program. This committee could be a subcommittee of the memorials or finance committee, or it could be a new committee created especially for this purpose. Large expenditures will not be necessary for this committee, but materials will be needed for education and promotion, and the board should make certain the committee is given the necessary resources to do its job.

3. *Become informed.* The committee first should educate itself on various planned giving options so that it can develop a plan to educate and promote these options within the congregation. Listed below is a review of the most common planned gifts for churches to promote:

Wills. The will is the most popular vehicle for making a planned gift. This should come as no surprise because the will is the best understood of all the planned giving instruments. Although not everyone has a will, most recognize the importance of one and realize that they should have one. Thus, promoting the will as a planned giving vehicle is relatively easy, and including the church when a will is made is also easy. The church can be remembered in three ways:

A fixed amount of money or a specific piece of property. A person can leave a stated amount of money or piece of property, such as a car, a home, or a farm to the church. This is a very simple way to remember the church in one's will.

A percentage of the estate. Dividing one's estate on a percentage basis is often the best way to remember the church and others in one's will. Using a percentage basis means that individuals and organizations included in the will share proportionately if the estate increases or decreases in value. Persons often find comfort in this method, as they never know what their assets will be when they die, but they do know that individuals and organizations will be remembered according to the proportions they have determined. A church might encourage its members to consider tithing their estates, just as it encourages them to practice proportionate giving during their lifetimes.

The residue. Whatever is left in an estate after specific bequests have been fulfilled is known as the residue. Persons can leave part or all of the residue to the church.

A person may choose to remember the church in one or more of these ways. For example, an individual could leave the church a book collection, a tithe of one's estate, and a portion of the residue.

If a person already has a will, often rewriting it is not necessary in order to include the church and its institutions. Rather, a simple codicil can be added to the will to modify the donor's intentions, thereby saving the expense of having a new will drawn up.

Gift annuities. Second only to the will in popularity as a planned giving vehicle is the gift annuity. A gift annuity is an agreement between an individual and an organization. The agreement stipulates that in return for a gift of money, the organization pays a fixed dollar

95

amount to one or two beneficiaries for life. In addition to benefitting the charitable organization, there are several benefits to the donor.

• The donor receives a charitable deduction for a portion of the gift.

• The beneficiary receives a guaranteed annual payment on the gift for life. The amount is determined by the age of the beneficiary at the time the annuity is prepared. Current rates of return vary from 6 percent for someone 35 years of age and under to 14 percent for someone 90 years of age and older. These rates are determined by the Conference on Gift Annuities, a national organization which establishes the guidelines for gift annuities.

• A portion of the annual payment is tax free, making the effective rate of return even higher than that noted above. Again, the amount that is free from income tax depends upon the beneficiary's age at the time the annuity is created, but generally ranges from 40 to 60 percent.

One can easily see why the gift annuity often is called the "mutually beneficial gift." Some individuals discover they can actually increase their own spendable income by taking out a gift annuity. For example, a person may have some securities which are paying a small dividend. The individual can purchase a gift annuity with these securities and, in turn, be guaranteed a higher annual payment for life. Or an individual may have money invested in a certificate of deposit which is paying less than an annuity would pay. When the certificate matures, the individual can take the proceeds and purchase an annuity with it, thus increasing spendable income.

Few churches are set up to write gift annuity agreements. However, many denominational foundations and church-related institutions can and do write such agreements, often for as small a gift as $1,000 or any amount above that. Thus, churches should promote gift annuities as appropriate planned giving vehicles and should work with their foundations or related institutions to offer these agreements to church members. The foundation or church-related institution would be responsible for holding and investing the funds and making payments to the beneficiary. Upon the death of the beneficiary the foundation or church-related institution would receive the remainder of the annuity, actuarially determined to be approximately 50 percent of the original amount.

Life insurance. An estimated 86 percent of American families own life insurance.[12] Thus, the potential for gifts of life insurance is great.

A gift of life insurance is also one of the simplest planned gifts to arrange, requiring no attorney or legal fees.

Life insurance can be given in several ways. Perhaps the easiest is to give the church an existing paid-up policy, which can be done simply by making the church the owner and beneficiary of the policy. A life insurance agent can assist in transferring policy ownership. Many people have existing policies which are no longer needed for their original purpose. They might find transferring policy ownership an especially attractive way to make a planned gift commitment. They can receive a charitable deduction in the year the gift is made either for the replacement cost of the policy or for the total paid for the policy, whichever is less.

Life insurance can be given even if premiums are still being paid. If the church is named irrevocable owner and beneficiary of the policy, the donor receives a charitable income tax deduction approximately equal to the cash surrender value at the time the gift is made. In addition, future premium payments can be deducted as charitable contributions.

Also, new life insurance policies can be purchased with the express purpose of naming the church irrevocable owner and beneficiary. Once again premium payments are deductible.

Persons also can name the church as a *co-beneficiary* of a policy, to share the proceeds with someone else; as a *secondary beneficiary,* to receive the proceeds if the first beneficiary has died; or as the *final beneficiary*. In addition, life insurance can be combined with other planned gift arrangements, such as trusts, to create estate plans which are beneficial to both families and charitable organizations. Most insurance agents are willing to provide detailed information on such plans.

Real estate. Some of the largest planned gifts to charities are gifts of real estate. A popular way to make a gift of real estate is through a life estate agreement. Here a home or farm is given, but the individual retains the right to live there and receive any income from the property for life. The individual receives an income tax deduction for a portion of the property's value, and the property passes directly to the organization upon the individual's death.

Persons also can make outright gifts of real estate or they can make such gifts through a will or a trust agreement. In some instances real estate can be given in return for life income. The variety of ways that persons can give real estate, according to their needs, makes it an attractive planned giving vehicle. Attorneys or others knowledgeable in gifts of real estate can help determine what is the best option for each individual.

Trusts. Trusts are legal contracts prepared by an attorney and tailored to an individual's needs and wishes. Charitable trusts are designed to benefit charity as well as the individual creating the trust. Such trusts can be revocable or irrevocable. If the trust is revocable, the donor can withdraw a portion or all of the principal if it is needed, but there are no income tax benefits. If the trust is irrevocable, there are income tax benefits.

Remainder trusts are the most common charitable trusts. The donor places money or property in a trust. The trustee in turn pays a specific annual amount to the donor and a survivor, if any. Upon the death of the survivor, the remainder of the trust assets goes to the named charity (hence, the name "charitable remainder trust"). Remainder trusts can be either annuity trusts (providing a fixed dollar amount annually) or unitrusts (providing a specified percentage of the market value of the trust assets, as valued annually). In either case the trust must pay the donor no less than 5 percent annually.

Numerous trust variations exist, and an attorney specializing in trusts should be consulted if a trust arrangement appears to be an attractive planned gift option.

At the same time that the planned giving committee seeks to educate itself on the various planned giving options, it should also educate itself on endowments and determine if the church would be well served by establishing an endowment fund. If the committee believes an endowment fund would be beneficial, it should work with the board in creating and approving such a fund.

4. *Prepare brochure.* The planned giving committee will next want to prepare a simple brochure to announce the planned giving program. The brochure should describe the purpose of the planned giving program and the endowment fund (if one is established), the major funding categories (such as mission fund, building fund, and general fund) to which members can give, and a brief description of each category. The brochure should describe how the fund will be administered and it should outline the various ways people can give. In addition to describing the various planned giving options, the brochure should note that outright gifts of cash, securities, and personal property are also welcomed. Finally the brochure should indicate who

should be contacted for further information or assistance in making a gift.

5. *Develop policies*. The committee should ensure that the appropriate structures are in place to manage the planned giving program with effectiveness and integrity. Is a written policy in place indicating how planned gifts will be received, invested, and managed? Is a system set up to ensure the maintenance and confidentiality of planned gift commitments? Are plans in place for regular reports to the congregation on commitments made, gifts received, and disbursement of funds? Answering these questions will help ensure that good management procedures are in place. Knowing that the church practices good management will help build confidence among members of the church's ability to be a responsible steward of planned gifts.

6. *Promote and educate*. The key to encouraging planned gift commitments will be the development of an active and continuous program of education and promotion. The education and promotion program should be low key and tasteful, but very much a part of the congregational life. Opportunities for education and promotion include, but are not limited to, the following:

Sermons. The planned giving committee should encourage the pastor to preach at least one sermon a year on the stewardship of accumulated resources. A number of myths about estate planning and charitable giving need to be dispelled, and the pulpit is a great place to address these myths.[13]

One such myth is that most estates are too small to remember the church. No estate is too small to make a witness. Even small planned gift commitments can make powerful statements about what is worthy of support and can encourage others to make commitments.

Another popular myth is that parents must leave their entire estates to their children. Remembering one's family is appropriate, but it does not follow that the best way to do so is by leaving them all of an estate. Numerous studies have shown that well-meaning parents rob children of initiative, discipline, harmony, and responsibility by leaving them entire estates. How much better if parents would seek to pass along their values as well as their riches. One couple did this by telling their four children they were going to consider the church as a fifth child and leave 20 percent of their estate to the church and church-related institutions.

A third myth is that it is okay to leave the church whatever is left over after other obligations have been addressed. Our Christian faith invites us to give God our firstfruits, not our leftovers. Does this not suggest that Christians should give their firstfruits in death as well as in life? How Christians dispose of their resources at the time of death will provide the world with one of the strongest statements of belief they will ever make.

Thus, preaching provides the opportunity to encourage church members to become faithful stewards in death as well as in life.

Seminars. Periodic seminars are excellent ways to educate congregational members about estate planning and planned giving. Some churches have had success in offering an initial seminar on financial planning to members and following this with seminars on topics of particular interest. For example, a seminar could be devoted to the topic of wills and their importance in an estate plan. Another seminar could focus on the importance of life insurance in one's financial planning. The primary purpose of such seminars is to provide a service to members in their financial and estate planning, but seminars also provide a low-key and effective way to remind persons of the opportunities available through these vehicles to remember the church. Oftentimes the leadership for these seminars can come from church members well versed in these areas, such as attorneys, life insurance agents, and financial planners. Such a meeting provides an effective way of further involving them in the ministry of the church.

Mailings. Quarterly or semiannual mailings of planned giving literature are recommended by experts as an effective way to educate members and identify those who are interested in more information. Church leaders must see such mailings as a continuous part of a planned giving program rather than a one-time effort, for lives of church members constantly are changing. A mailing about wills may mean nothing to an individual the first time. Six months later a similar mailing might spark interest in that individual, for perhaps a birth, a marriage, or a death has taken place—all of which can make a person more receptive to considering a will.

Professionally written planned giving brochures are available for purchase and can be personalized with the church's name and address. These can be sent to members along with a cover letter and response card for requesting more information.

Blurbs. In addition to regular mailings, the planned giving committee should place articles in the church newsletter from time to time, highlighting planned giving opportunities. One-sentence statements could also provide occasional filler in church bulletins. The committee may choose to promote planned giving in all church publications. One church, for example, printed the simple statement, "Remember the church in your will," on its stationery and all of its printed materials. Today that church receives thousands of dollars annually in bequest income.

Literature. Planned giving literature should be displayed prominently in the church. A rack, featuring brochures, books, and sample forms for different planned giving arrangements, might be placed in a high-traffic area. A section in the library could be devoted to planned giving materials. Planned giving committee members might highlight this literature in a special display in the church's lobby on an annual basis. As new planned giving materials are received, reviews could be written and included in the church newsletter.

Visits. The visit plays an important role in planned giving, just as it does in annual giving and capital giving. Those persons who express an interest in planned giving through any of the above activities should be visited if possible to determine how the church can be of further assistance. The purpose of the visit is not to push for a commitment, but to help persons determine what they want to do with their resources and to assist them in finding the right people to make their goals a reality. These visits can be made by the pastor or by a layperson especially trained in this area. In the long run the church's planned giving program will benefit from this service-oriented approach.

7. *Provide recognition.* A final step for the planned giving committee is to develop a recognition program for those who remember the church with a planned gift commitment. The purpose of a recognition program is twofold: to thank personally those who have made such commitments, rather than waiting to thank the executor of their estate, and to encourage others to consider making similar commitments.

Annually the church should recognize those persons who have made planned gift commitments within the past year. These persons could be introduced at a worship service and presented with a personalized plaque or other memento. Such mementoes, displayed in the home, can become conversation pieces, providing an opportunity for individuals to share what they have done and to invite others to join them.

Another appropriate way to show recognition is to print annually a pamphlet or brochure which lists all of those who have made planned gift commitments to the church. As church members see this growing list, some will be moved to make their own commitments.

One church has formed a special group, named the Wesley Associates, which includes all of those who have made planned gift commitments to the church. A brochure explains that the name "Wesley Associates" is derived from John Wesley's famous sermon of 1706 when he admonished the parishioners to "earn all you can, save all you can, give all you can." This church recognizes Wesley Associates as persons who have earned a living, saved what they could, and now seek to give what they can through planned gifts to glorify God. The brochure suggests that the Wesley Associates group is both a symbol and an inspiration. The group symbolizes the importance the church places on this kind of commitment and also seeks to inspire others to join.

The brochure, entitled "An Invitation to Become a Wesley Associate," explains that membership is open to anyone who has made provision for the church through a will, an annuity, an insurance policy, a gift of real estate, or a trust arrangement. Persons are invited to let the church know if they have made such arrangements or if they would like further information on planned giving options. These brochures are placed in the literature racks and annually sent out in the church newsletter.

Each year the Wesley Associates are invited to a special dinner where new members are introduced and presented with a gift of appreciation. The greatest gift for most, however, is knowing they are part of a group which is playing a significant role in strengthening the future of the church.

And that, of course, is the goal of an effective planned giving program. This goal is available to every church willing to develop this part of its stewardship emphasis.

TO SUMMARIZE

The third component of a well-developed church giving program is planned giving. In most churches it has received the least attention. As a result, churches lag behind other charitable organizations in dollars received through planned gifts.

The benefits of a planned giving program are many. Planned giving provides an opportunity to witness to one's faith at death and to strengthen the future ministries of the church. A planned giving program enables persons to make larger gifts than otherwise possible and to establish living memorials. Planned gifts offer donors many benefits, including the possibility of income for life, income tax deductions, reduction of federal estate taxes, and professional management of assets. A planned giving program also enhances a church's annual and capital giving.

An effective planned giving program needs to be proactive. Approval should be obtained and a committee appointed to develop and manage a planned giving program of education and promotion.

The committee should begin its work by learning about the major planned giving options. It should also decide if an endowment fund is desirable for the church and should develop appropriate structures and policies for managing the program.

The success of the planned giving program will be determined by how consistently and effectively it is promoted within the church. Opportunities for education include sermons, periodic seminars, regular mailings, articles and other blurbs, readily available literature within the church, and personal visits.

The final element in an effective program is appropriate recognition of those who have made planned gift commitments. Such recognition should highlight the importance the church places on this kind of giving, and should inspire others to make planned gift commitments.

An effective planned giving program can be readily implemented by any church.

Chapter Eight

A CONCLUDING WORD
TO CHURCH LEADERS

"No organization is stronger than the quality of its leadership, or ever extends its constituency far beyond the degree to which its leadership is representative."

Edgar D. Powell[1]

The previous chapters have provided a basic overview of the fundamentals of fund raising and have shown how these might be utilized by the church to develop effective annual, capital, and planned giving programs.

Harold Seymour has likened these three programs to a three-legged stool. Milk stools, he notes, always have three legs which enable the stool to remain stable no matter what the terrain is. He suggests that in order for institutions to remain stable, they too should have the three fund raising programs in place. Any institution that does not have all three legs in place simply has an incomplete program and risks instability. Any person, he concludes, can give annually, can make occasional capital gifts, and can make a planned gift to help ensure the institution's future.[2]

The challenge to church leaders is to make sure that all three programs are in place, properly understood and supported by the congregation, adequately staffed and managed by volunteers and committees, and regularly promoted by the pastor and key laypersons. At first this task may seem overwhelming, consisting of endless task forces, committee meetings, brochures, and policy statements. How does a church begin?

A beginning point might be to have the key church leaders individually read this book and then come together to discuss the following questions:

- Is there an interest in having this church grow in biblical stewardship?
- Are we willing to develop a program of continuous stewardship education?
- Are we willing to commit our resources of time, talent, and energy to develop effective programs of annual, capital, and planned giving?
- Are we willing to model a growing understanding of stewardship of financial resources in our own personal lives?

If the answers to the above questions are positive, the church is in good shape to move forward. On the other hand, if key leaders are hesitant or negative in their responses to the above, the church may not be prepared to move ahead. Edgar Powell is correct: "No organization is stronger than the quality of its leadership." To move a congregation beyond its leadership is nearly impossible. Wallace Fisher puts it well when he writes, "Until the ordained and elected lay leaders of a congregation are themselves persuaded by the gospel and the evidences of human need in this world to do generous, proportionate, and disciplined giving, it is not likely that the congregation (except for a family here and there) will give really serious thought to a biblical stewardship of their possessions. The bland can lead the bland, but only to be more bland."[3]

Wallace suggests that those leaders not willing to grow in doing stewardship should, as an act of simple integrity, surrender their positions to other persons who are willing. He further suggests that if a congregation cannot find enough key leaders for its board who are seeking to grow in responsible stewardship, it should ask itself whether it has a right to function as a congregation.[4]

Some may find Wallace's words unduly severe. As painful as they may be, they are accurate. Ultimately the success of any fund raising program—and the strength of any church—is not dependent on strategies, policies, tools, or techniques, but on leadership. Leaders must be willing to study, learn, and grow in stewardship understanding and commitment. They must be willing to act boldly on their beliefs and to seek to model Christian stewardship to others.

Each church will need to find appropriate ways to address the question of leadership and ensure that leaders are in place who are willing and eager to move the church forward in stewardship. Once this is done, leaders can develop a timeline that fits the local church's situation for instituting the three essential giving components. To introduce all three programs at once would be foolish and overwhelming to everyone. The following is one model of how a church might introduce the three giving programs over a five-year period. Church leaders should feel free to adapt this model or to create their own.

Year One

● Church board adopts statement of commitment to develop a comprehensive stewardship of financial resources program and appoints planning committee and stewardship committee.
● Planning committee develops mission statement, assesses the environment, and begins formulating long-range and short-term goals.
● Stewardship committee prepares plan for long-term stewardship education program.
● Appropriate committees are formed to conduct annual giving program.

Year Two

● Planning committee continues to formulate long-range goals, and updates short-term goals.
● Stewardship committee continues to oversee stewardship education program.
● New committees are formed to conduct annual giving program.
● Planned giving committee is appointed to launch planned giving program.

Year Three

● Planning committee updates long-range plan. Initial work is begun for a capital campaign if important capital needs are identified and annual giving is strong.
● Stewardship education program continues.
● Planned giving education/promotion continues.
● Annual giving program continues.

Year Four

- Campaign steering committee is formed and leadership gifts sought for capital campaign.
- Stewardship education program continues.
- Planned giving education/promotion continues.
- Annual giving program continues.

Year Five

- Capital campaign publicly launched, conducted, and concluded.
- Stewardship education program continues.
- Planned giving education/promotion continues.
- Annual giving program continues.

We end where we began—by affirming that resource development is an essential part of ministry today. Developing a strong stewardship of financial resources program is a responsibility that has been placed on church leaders, a responsibility which cannot be neglected if they are to be faithful in fulfilling the mission of the church. The time to begin is now.

ENDNOTES

CHAPTER ONE

[1] Raymond B. Knudsen, *New Models for Financing the Local Church* (New York: Association Press, 1974), p. 65.

[2] The author actually visited these three pastors in 1988. The names have been changed; the situations described in the narrative are factual.

[3] *Giving USA: The Annual Report on Philanthropy for the Year 1987* (Albany: Boyd Printing Co., 1988), p. 75.

[4] Ibid.

[5] John L. and Sylvia Ronsvalle, *A Comparison of the Growth in Church Contributions with United States Per Capita Income* (Champaign, Illinois: empty tomb, inc., 1988), p. 4.

[6] Ibid., pp. 131-32.

CHAPTER TWO

[1] Douglas W. Johnson, *The Tithe: Challenge or Legalism?* (Nashville: Abingdon Press, 1984), p. 80.

[2] Robert F. Sharpe, *Before You Give Another Dime* (Nashville: Thomas Nelson Publishers, 1979), pp. 26-30.

[3] Albert Edward Day, *Discipline and Discovery* (Nashville: Parthenon Press, 1961), p. 81.

[4] Joe W. Walker, *Money in the Church* (Nashville: Abingdon, 1982), p. 83.

[5] H. Richard Niebuhr, *The Purpose of the Church and Its Ministry* (New York: Harper & Row, 1956), p. 27.

[6] Johnson, *The Tithe: Challenge or Legalism?*, p. 82.

[7] J. David Schmidt, "Where Does the Money Go?", *Fund Raising Management*, July 1987, p. 67.

[8] Walker, *Money in the Church*, p. 106.

[9] Charles Moore, *Daniel H. Burnham: Architect, Planner of Cities*, II (Boston: Houghton-Mifflin Company, 1921), p. 147.

CHAPTER THREE

[1]Mother Teresa of Calcutta, *A Gift for God* (New York: Harper & Row, 1975), p. 77.

[2]T. A. Kantonen, *A Theology for Christian Stewardship* (Philadelphia: Muhlenberg Press, 1956), p. 24.

[3]G. T. Smith, "Presidential and Trustee Leadership in Fund Raising" (paper presented to the Council for Advancement and Support of Education, San Francisco, CA, April 20-22, 1988), p. 3.

[4]Henry A. Rosso, "Successful Philanthropy: The Comprehensive Resources Development Program" (paper presented to the Association of Theological Schools Development Seminar, San Francisco, CA, April 16-19, 1989), p. 6.

[5]James Gregory Lord, *The Raising of Money: Thirty-Five Essentials Every Trustee Should Know* (Cleveland, Ohio: Third Sector Press, 1988), pp. 3-4.

[6]Virginia A. Hodgkinson and Murray S. Weitzman, *Giving and Volunteering in the United States: Summary of Findings from a National Survey* (Washington, D.C.: Independent Sector, 1988), p. 6.

[7]Ibid., p. 10.

[8]Clarence W. Tompkins, *Born a Promoter* (Lake Mills, Iowa: Graphics Publishing Co., Inc., 1984), p. 5.

CHAPTER FOUR

[1]*Accent on Philanthropy II*, p. 15.

[2]Dennis J. Murray, *The Guaranteed Fund-Raising System* (Boston, Massachusetts: American Institute of Management, 1987), p. 163.

[3]Philip Kotler, *Marketing for Nonprofit Organizations* (2nd ed.; Englewood Cliffs, New Jersey: Prentice-Hall, Inc., 1982), pp. 86-87.

[4]Ibid., p. 85.

[5]*Bulletin on Public Relations and Development for Colleges and Universities* (Chicago, IL.: Gonser Gerber Tinker Stuhr, January, 1986), p. 2.

CHAPTER FIVE

[1]Walker, *Money in the Church,* p. 113.

[2]Manfred Holck, Jr., *Church Finance in a Complex Economy* (Nashville: Abingdon Press, 1983), p. 73.

[3]Paul H. Virts, "Public Perceptions of Christian Fund-Raising Ethics," *Fund Raising Management,* July 1987, p. 44.

[4]Charlie W. Shedd, *How to Develop a Tithing Church* (Nashville: Abingdon Press, 1961).

[5]Eugene L. Brand, "The Offering: Theory and Practice," in *Teaching and Preaching Stewardship,* ed. by Nordan C. Murphy (New York: National Council of Churches, 1985), p. 45.

[6]Herbert Mather, *Becoming a Giving Church* (Nashville: Discipleship Resources, 1985), p. 38.

[7]Holck, *Church Finance in a Complex Economy,* p. 56.

[8]Harold J. Seymour, *Designs for Fund-Raising* (New York: McGraw-Hill Book Company, 1966), p. 150.

[9]Scott G. Nichols, "Annual Giving Programs: Responding to New Trends and Realities," in *Handbook of Institutional Advancement,* ed. by A. Westley Rowland (2nd ed.; San Francisco: Jossey-Bass Publishers, 1986), p. 259.

[10]Ibid., p. 260.

[11]Seymour, *Designs for Fund-Raising,* p. 151.

[12]Quoted in Holck, *Church Finance in a Complex Economy,* p. 74.

[13]Nichols, "Annual Giving Programs: Responding to New Trends and Realities," p. 261.

[14]William W. How, "We Give Thee But Thine Own," *The Methodist Hymnal* (Nashville: Methodist Publishing House, 1966), p. 181.

[15]Minneapolis *Star Tribune,* November 25, 1988, p. 4B.

CHAPTER SIX

[1]Thomas E. Broce, *Fund Raising,* 2nd ed. (Norman, OK: University of Oklahoma Press, 1987), p. 44.

[2]Adapted from *Bulletin on Public Relations and Development for Colleges and Universities* (Chicago, IL.: Gonser Gerber Tinker Stuhr, March 1986), p. 3.

[3]Seymour, *Designs for Fund-Raising,* p. 87.
[4]Quoted in Broce, *Fund Raising,* p. 53.
[5]Ibid., p. 50.
[6]Seymour, *Designs for Fund-Raising,* p. 50.
[7]John D. Rockefeller, Jr., "The Technique of Soliciting," *Winning Words: A Volunteer's Guide to Asking for Major Gifts* (Washington, D.C.: Council for Advancement and Support of Education, 1984), pp. 4-5.

CHAPTER SEVEN

[1]Raymond B. Knudsen, *New Models for Financing the Local Church,* p. 120.
[2]Theodore P. Hurwitz, "Designing and Managing Planned Giving Programs," *Handbook of Institutional Advancement,* ed. by A. Westley Rowland (2nd ed.; San Francisco: Jossey-Bass Publishers, 1986), p. 311.
[3]Robert F. Sharpe, *Before You Give Another Dime,* p. 120.
[4]Knudsen, *New Models for Financing the Local Church,* p. 120.
[5]Johnson, *The Tithe: Challenge or Legalism?,* p. 93.
[6]"Planned Gifts: 31% of Individual Gifts to Higher Education," *Give & Take: News and Ideas for Development Executives of Nonprofit Institutions,* January 1989, p. 1.
[7]*Giving USA: The Annual Report on Philanthropy for the Year 1987,* p. 39.
[8]Knudsen, *New Models for Financing the Local Church,* p. 54.
[9]Quoted in Fern Underwood, ed., *The Skeptic and the Spirit* (Board of Laity & Stewardship, 1985), p. 47.
[10]Ibid., p. 49.
[11]*1988 Annual Report of the Wesley United Methodist Church's Fellheimer Trust,* pp. 1-3.
[12]Robert F. Sharpe, *27 Plus Ways to Increase Giving to Your Church* (Memphis: National Planned Giving Publishers, 1986), p. 71.
[13]David L. Heetland, "Remembering the Church at Death," *Circuit Rider* (April 1986), p. 13.

CHAPTER EIGHT

[1]*Accent on Philanthropy II,* p. 11.

[2]Seymour, *Designs for Fund-Raising,* pp. 109-10.

[3]Wallace E. Fisher, *All the Good Gifts: On Doing Biblical Steward-ship* (Minneapolis: Augsburg Publishing House, 1979), p. 71.

[4]Ibid., pp. 72-73.

ANNOTATED BIBLIOGRAPHY

Barrett, Wayne C. *The Church Finance Idea Book*. Nashville: Discipleship Resources, 1989. Order no. DR065B.
An encyclopedia of proven ideas and personal experiences in local church finance.

Barry, Bryan W. *Strategic Planning Workbook for Nonprofit Organizations*. Minneapolis: Amherst H. Wilder Foundation, 1986.
A helpful workbook containing examples and worksheets, designed to guide organizations through a step-by-step planning process.

Berger, Hilbert J. *Now, Concerning the Offering*. Nashville: Discipleship Resources, 1987. Order no. ST066K.
A booklet which stresses the importance of the offering and provides sample offering sentences and prayers.

Fisher, Wallace E. *All the Good Gifts: On Doing Biblical Stewardship*. Minneapolis: Augsburg Publishing House, 1979.
Designed as a study for church boards, this book focuses on the meaning of biblical stewardship and includes discussion questions.

Gaskill, Norma W. *Putting God First: The Tithe*. Nashville: Discipleship Resources, 1988. Order no. DR058B.
A helpful booklet which invites persons to explore the importance of the tithe through biblical reflection, personal testimonies, journaling, and group study.

————— . *There's Joy in Caring: Leader's Guide for a Study of Stewardship*. Nashville: Discipleship Resources, 1985. Order no. ST047K.
This booklet offers guidance for preparing and leading an eight-session course on the meaning of stewardship, based on the United Methodist "Foundation Statement for Christian Stewardship."

Because God Gives. Nashville: Discipleship Resources, 1987. Order no. ST064K.
A booklet of selected scripture passages about four significant areas of giving.

Annotated Bibliography

Holck, Manfred, Jr. *Church Finance in a Complex Economy.* Nashville: Abingdon Press, 1983.
A look at some creative ways church leaders can finance ministry in an inflationary society.

Johnson, Douglas W. *The Tithe: Challenge or Legalism?* Nashville: Abingdon Press, 1984.
A serious study which encourages the reader to view giving as a way of life.

————. *The Tithe: Challenge or Legalism? Leader's Guide.* Nashville: Discipleship Resources, 1984. Order no. ST031B.
A guide to assist church leaders in preparing a six-session group study of the book by the same title.

Kincaid, J. LaVon, Sr. *Thanks*Giving: Stewardship Sermons out of the Ethnic Minority Experience.* Nashville: Discipleship Resources, 1984. Order no. DR007B.
A collection of sixteen stewardship sermons from a variety of Christian ethnic traditions.

Knudsen, Raymond B. *Developing Dynamic Stewardship.* Nashville: Abingdon, 1978.
A collection of fifteen sermons on commitment and giving.

————. *New Models for Financing the Local Church.* New York: Association Press, 1974.
A good review of some traditional and emerging ways to finance the church's ministries.

Lord, James Gregory. *The Raising of Money: Thirty-Five Essentials Every Trustee Should Know.* Cleveland: Third Sector Press, 1988.
An easily read book which seeks to give volunteers the skills needed to seek major gifts.

Mather, Herbert. *Becoming a Giving Church.* Nashville: Discipleship Resources, 1985. Order no. DR023B.
A booklet designed to help church leaders discover the joy and excitement of giving.

Mather, Herbert and Joiner, Donald W. *Celebrate Giving.* Nashville: Discipleship Resources, 1988. Order no. ST073K.
A manual that outlines a ten-week financial commitment campaign, including planning a calendar and job descriptions and writing letters.

115

Murphy, Nordan C., ed. *Teaching and Preaching Stewardship: An Anthology.* New York: National Council of the Churches of Christ in the U.S.A., 1985.
A collection of the most memorable addresses presented at events sponsored by the Commission on Stewardship of the National Council of Churches.

Sharpe, Robert F. *Before You Give Another Dime.* Nashville: Thomas Nelson Publishers, 1979.
An excellent book which describes numerous ways to give more effectively.

_____ . *The Planned Giving Idea Book.* Nashville: Thomas Nelson Publishers, 1980.
A valuable reference book for churches with planned giving programs.

Shedd, Charlie W. *How To Develop a Tithing Church.* Nashville: Abingdon Press, 1961.
Shedd's book provides a classic description of a year-round stewardship education program. Out of print.

Underwood, Fern, ed. *The Skeptic and the Spirit.* Board of Laity & Stewardship, 1985.
This book is packed with illustrations of stewardship at work within the Iowa Annual Conference of The United Methodist Church.

Walker, Joe W. *Money in the Church.* Nashville: Abingdon, 1982.
Walker compares former and present patterns of giving in The United Methodist Church, and encourages leaders to regard discussions of money as holy talk.

Winning Words: A Volunteer's Guide to Asking for Major Gifts. Washington, D.C.: Council for Advancement and Support of Education, 1984.
Only eight pages long, this brochure is packed with suggestions that will give volunteers confidence in inviting gifts from others.

Get $30.00 worth of books
FREE!

When you subscribe to the **Discipleship Resources Subscription
Service** you receive **$60.00 worth** of books for your **$30.00**
subscription price.
We will send you or your church organization from one to four brand new
resources every other month for an entire year from
the eight program sections of **The General
Board of Discipleship.**
These resources (books, booklets, brochures, tracts, informational
pieces, etc.) were written and produced solely to help
the local church pastor and lay leaders in their
ministries dealing with:

**Evangelism
Christian Education
Worship
Stewardship
Ministry of the Laity
Ethnic Local Church
Concerns
United Methodist Men
Covenant Discipleship**

Additional copies of resources that you find to be particularly helpful in
your ministry can also be purchased with special subscriber coupons at
20% off the regular price. What better/more inexpensive way is there
to equip the leaders and committee members of your church with
the tools they need to conduct their vital ministries
in the name of Jesus Christ.

☐ **Yes, please enroll me for a one year subscription for just $30.00.**

Bill to:	Ship to:
Name _____	**Name** _____
Address _____	**Address** _____
City/St/Zp _____	**City/St/Zp** _____

☐ **Payment enclosed**   ☐ **Bill me later**

Clip out this order blank and mail to:
DISCIPLESHIP RESOURCES, 1908 Grand Avenue. P.O. Box 189. Nashville, TN 37202
or call us at **(615) 340-7284.**